# 目 录

前　言　　　　　　　　1

第一封信　　　　　　49

第二封信　　　　　　67

第三封信　　　　　　91

第四封信　　　　　　97

第五封信　　　　　　123

第六封信　　　　　　153

第七封信　　　　　　177

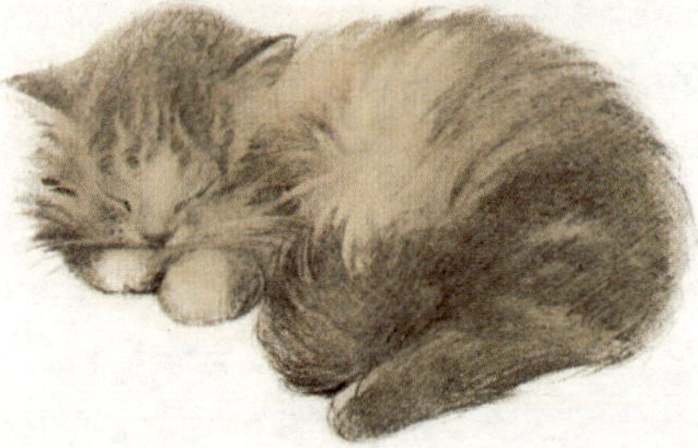

# 前　　言

亲爱的孩子们：

我并不十分肯定是我的小猫咪自己写了这些信。这些信总是夹在我妈妈或是其他朋友给我写的信当中，我在家的时候，从来都没有看到过小猫咪写东西。但是这些信的笔迹太糟糕了，而且全都签着小猫咪的名字。每当我问起的时候，妈妈总是神神秘秘的，就像是这里面藏着什么惊天秘密一样。所以在我长大之前，我从来都没有怀疑过是小猫咪在天黑之后独自悄悄写了这些信。

这些信是在我还是个很小很小的小姑娘的时候写的，当时我跟爸爸出门度假。我们坐着自家的马

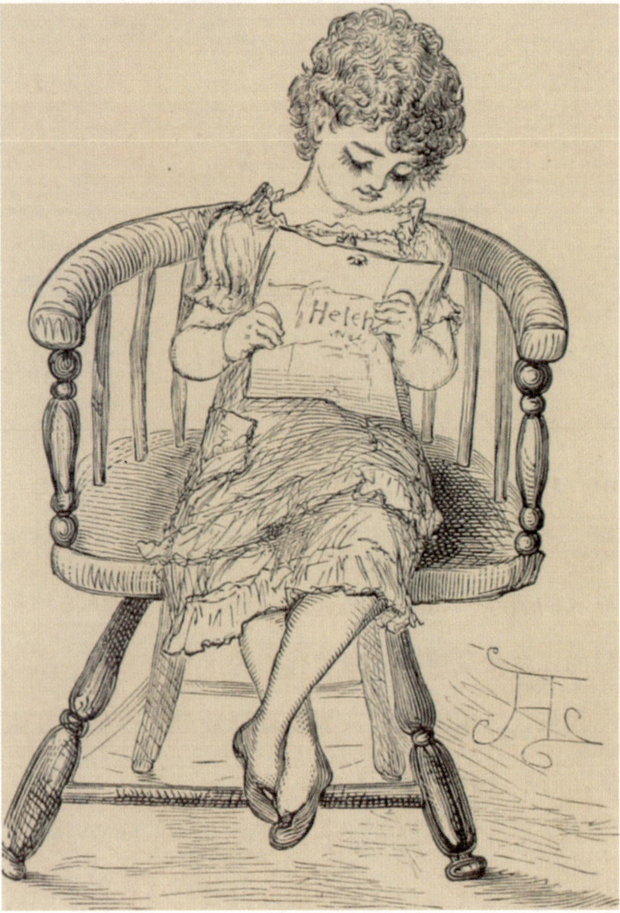

车去旅行,这是我记忆中最快乐的事情之一。我和爸爸的衣服都装在一个小皮包里,用皮带吊在马车下面。一路上,车轮滚滚向前,而小皮包不停摇摆,前前后后,晃晃悠悠。遇到陡峭的山,爸爸和我总是自己爬上去,因为我们的马——老查雷的身体不怎么壮实。走在马车后面的时候,我的眼睛一直盯着那个皮包。我觉得,这么携带皮包可是最不安全的方式,我非常希望我最好的衣服能包在包袱里,由我自己抱在大腿上。这是我在旅途中唯一不快乐的地方——我很担心那个皮包会在我们没有注意的时候掉下去,落在路上,当我到达姑妈家的时候,就再也没有任何漂亮衣服穿了。但一路上,那皮包都很安全,住在姑妈家期间,每天下午我都能扬扬得意地穿上我最美的裙子。我那时候可真傻,居然花那么多心思在这样的事情上面。

  在到达姑妈家后的第四天,我收到了妈妈寄来的一封信，里面写了一大堆行为指南，其中夹着来自小猫咪的第一封信。我一直把这两封信装在我的罩裙口袋里面，因为这是我第一次收到信，很是为此骄傲。我向所有人显摆这两封信，大家全都因为小猫的信笑得很厉害，问我是否真的相信小猫自己能写信。我觉得，也许是我妈妈握着她的爪子，帮她拿着笔，因为妈妈有时候也会握着我的手，引导着我的笔写下一些词语。我请爸爸在给妈妈的信里面帮忙问问她，小猫咪的信是不是这样写出来的。但是妈妈给爸爸的第二封信寄来时，他把里面这句话读给我听，"告诉海伦，我没有握着小猫咪的爪子写信。"所以，我确信是小猫自己写了信，就如同我刚才说过的，直到长大后，我才开始怀疑这件事。你们得明白，对我来说，我的小猫咪是只了不起的小猫咪，她做什么都不稀奇。我很清楚通常猫都不会读，不会写，但是，我觉得我的小猫咪是世界上独

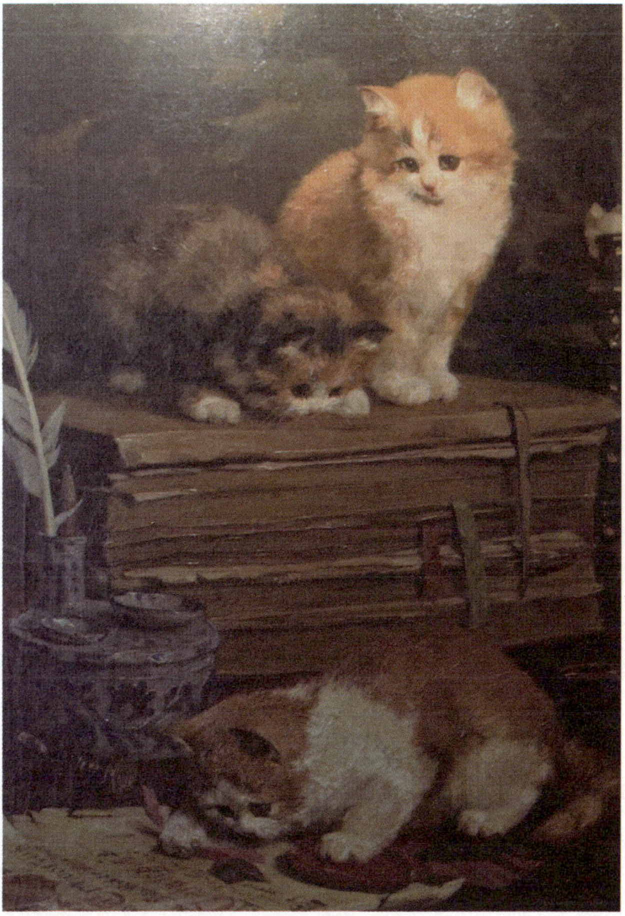

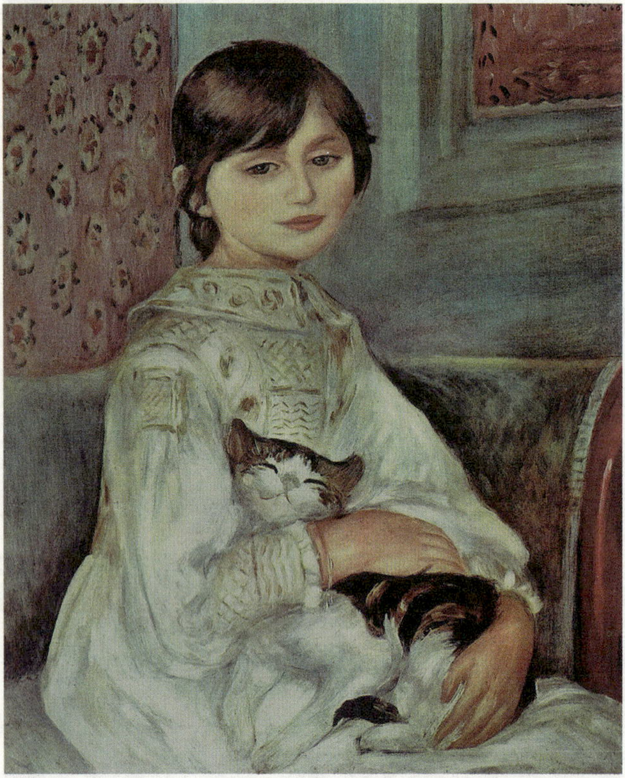

一无二的。小猫已经死去很多年了，但时至今日，她的样子依然会清晰地出现在我的眼前，就如同昨天我还看到她活生生的一样。

我刚开始养她的时候，她还是一只小猫崽，但她长得很快，没多久，就比我希望的大了。我希望她能一直小小的。她的皮毛是美丽的深灰色，侧面有黑色的条纹，就像老虎身上的条纹一样。她的眼睛非常大，耳朵又长又尖，与众不同。她看上去像只狐狸，而且她非常聪明，非常淘气，所以有些人认为她肯定有狐狸的血统。她常常做一件我从来都没有听说别的猫会做的事情：她经常玩捉迷藏。你听说过猫玩捉迷藏吗？而最神奇的地方是，她完全是自发自愿地玩的。每天中午，我放学回家，她一听到我关上院子大门，就会卖力地跑上楼梯，站在楼梯顶上，从那里透过栏杆缝隙往下看。当我打开门的时候，她会发出一声可爱而轻微的喵喵叫声，那声音有些像大猫呼唤自己的小猫崽时候的叫声。我一踏上楼梯，走上去找她，她就会以最快的速度跑开，藏到一张床底下。当我走入房间内，根本看不到小猫咪在哪里。如果我叫她，她会从床底下钻出来。但如果我什么话都不说，离开房间下楼去，不到一分钟，她就会飞速回到楼梯顶部的位置上，再次发出那特别的喵喵声。只要我一出现，她就会立刻跑开，像刚才一样藏到床底。有时候，她会这么反复三四次。向外人展示她的这个小把戏，是我妈妈的一项特别的娱乐活动。不过，很奇怪，如果她观察到有其他人在看，就绝不会做第二次。我叫她的时候，她会从床底下出来，如果有陌生人看着，她就会以娴雅的姿态直直地向我走来，似乎她会在床底下只不过是个单纯的巧合，不管我做什么、说什么，她当天都不会再嬉闹了。

　　不管我去哪里，她总是爱跟着我，就像只小狗

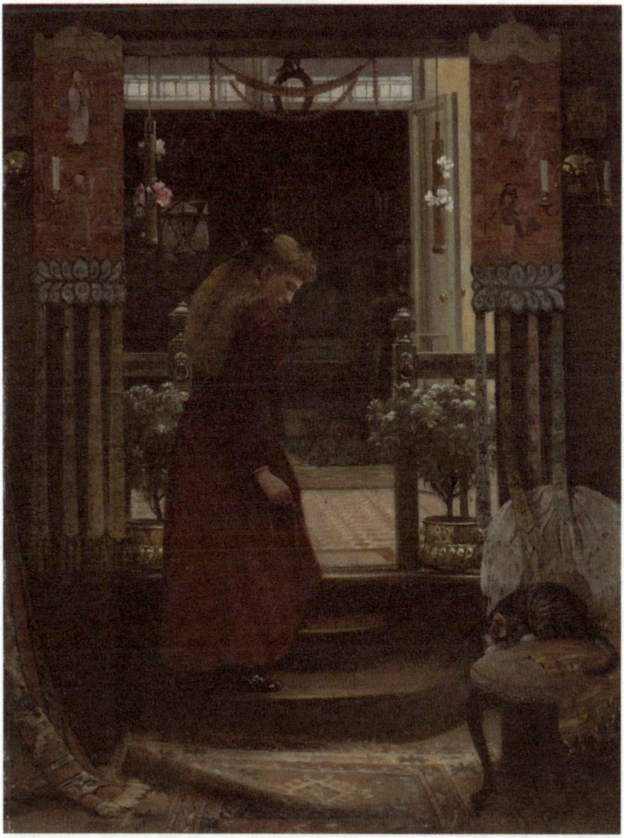

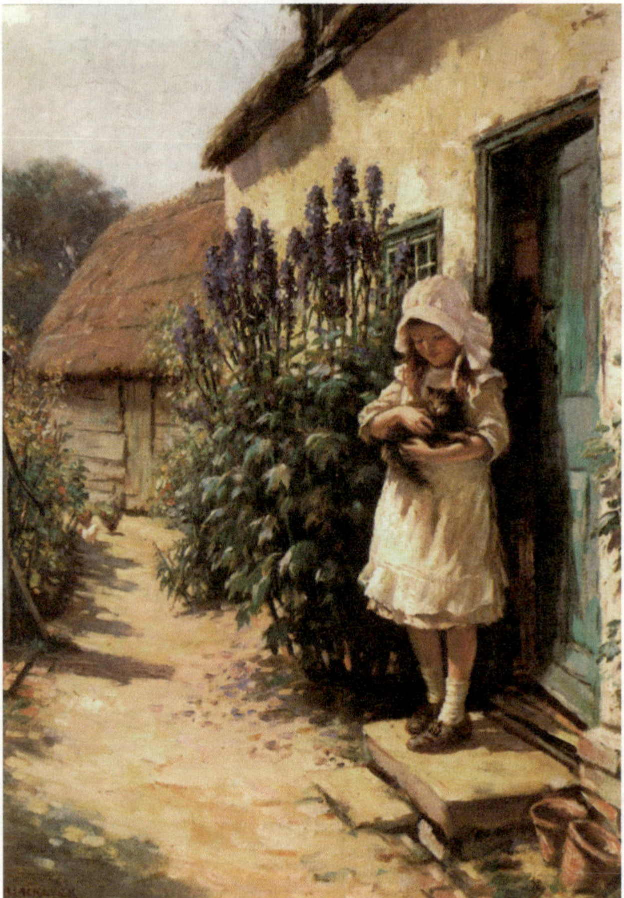

一样。她每天都跟着我去学校。星期天的时候，想要她不跟着我们去教堂，真要费很大力气。有一次，她跟着我去了，好多人看到她都笑了，尽管那场合并不适合笑，他们本来都感到很悲伤。因为那是一个大学教授的葬礼。

教授的家人都坐在一起。到时间了，他们要离开教堂上车去往墓地，人们按照姓名排序，一个接一个地上前去安慰他们。当轮到我们家的时候，爸爸妈妈手挽着手走在前面，姐姐和我跟在他们后面，再后面，是非常郑重的一个，那就是我的小猫，她之前跟着我偷偷溜进了教堂，谁也没有注意到她。她的步伐缓慢而慎重，径直跟在我和姐姐的身后，仿佛她也是我们家的一员。实际上，她确实是。人们开始微笑。我们穿过前门走下台阶，站在那里的一些男人和男孩都笑出了声。我不感到惊奇，因为那画面肯定非常滑稽。又过了一秒，有人跳过来，抓住了小猫。她叫得可真是凄厉啊!然后,她用爪子抓了那个人的脸,所以那人很快就将她放了下来。我一听到她的声音就转过身,低声唤她。她飞快地跑到我身边,我抱起她,一直抱着她走完了剩下的路。我甚至看到爸爸妈妈也都笑了一下,虽然只有一小下。这是小猫咪参加过的唯一一次葬礼。

小猫咪在这些信中所写的事情发生之后又活了好几年。

在掉进肥皂桶的可怕经历之后很久,小猫咪才再次长出毛来。她的毛最终还是长了出来,看起来就和从前一样。没有人能看出来她遭遇过什么,不过她的眼神变得很差。她的眼角一直都没有痊愈,可怜的小猫咪经常坐着揉眼睛,一揉就是好几个钟头。有时候,她用爪子每揉一下眼睛,都会喵喵叫着,抬头看我的脸,仿佛在说:"你看不出来我的眼睛有多酸吗?为什么你不为我做点儿什么呢?"

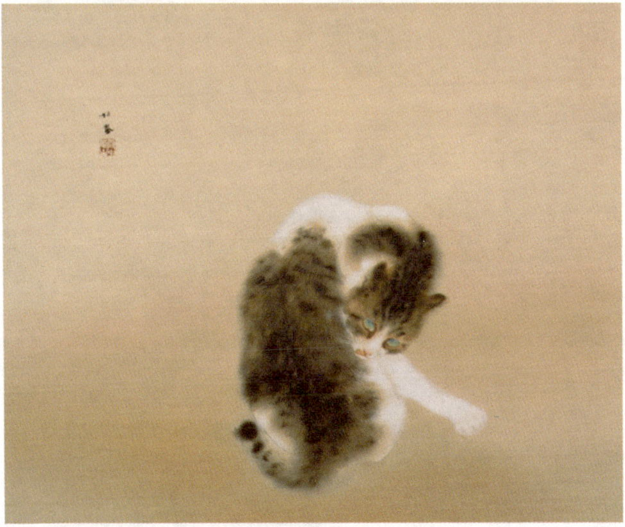

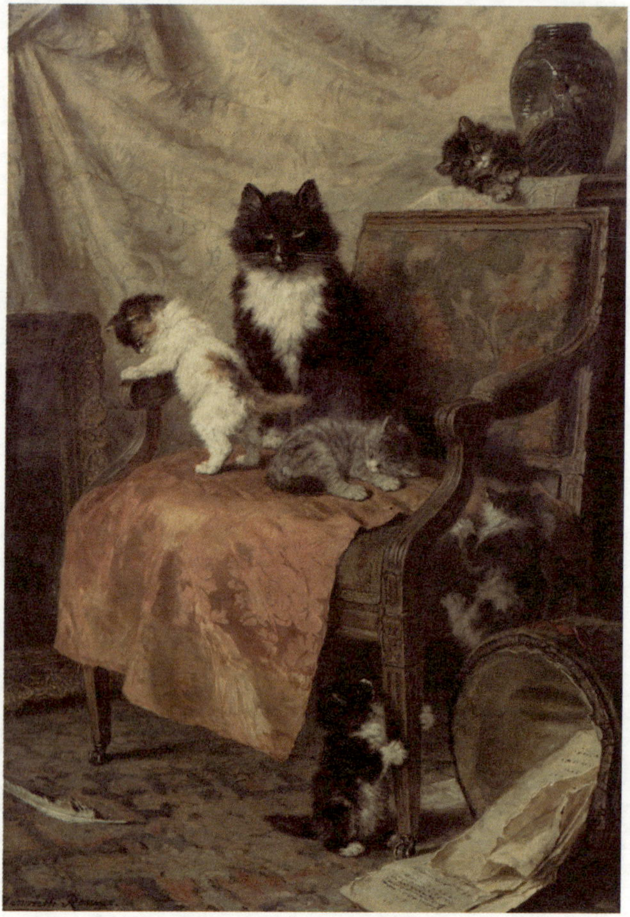

自从遭遇了那场意外,她就再也没有办法做一个捕鼠者了,也不太玩耍了。我记得有一天听到妈妈对别人说:"小猫在摇篮里面那几天被宠坏了,我肯定她希望后半辈子都被人摇着。她一看到硬牛肉,就鼻子朝天,那样子实在太可笑了。真不应该让她吃里脊肉!"

最后,由于营养充足但缺乏锻炼,小猫咪变得越来越胖,变成了一个庞然大物,而且越来越懒惰,除了蜷着身子躺在软垫子上什么也不愿意做。

她的个子已经太大了,没有办法再卧在我的小椅子里了。那椅子里本来放了一个绿色的波纹布垫子,小猫在上面睡了很多年,我自己很少用那个椅子,因为她在里面的时间太多了。但后来,这个椅子对她来说太狭窄了,她便开始占据整个房子中她能找到的最舒适的地方,有时候是沙发,有时候是扶手椅,有时候是某个人的床尾。但是无论她在哪里，肯定都是刚好碍事的位置。那可怜的小家伙，不是被头朝下丢下扶手椅，就是被匆匆地赶下沙发，或是不断地被赶下床。最后她终于搞懂了，看到有人走向她正躺着的椅子、沙发或是床时，最聪明的做法就是赶快离开。她带着受伤而充满责备的表情，缓缓地站起来，伸展四肢，去寻找下一个可以安睡的地方，这情景真的非常滑稽。房子里的每个人都不喜欢看到她，只有我例外，我曾经为了她多次和女仆发生过激烈争吵。甚至是我妈妈，她本来是我认识的最和蔼的人，最后也终于对小猫咪失去了耐心。有一天，她对我说：

"海伦，你的猫太老了，也太胖了，她自己不舒服，对其他人来说也是大麻烦，我觉得让她安乐死比较好。"

"杀了我的小猫？"我叫道，然后号啕大哭，声音又大又尖，我猜我妈妈也被吓到了，因为她很快

便回答说:

"不要害怕,亲爱的,除非万不得已,否则我们不会那么做的。如果小猫一直都很不舒服,你肯定也不会希望她痛苦下去。"

"她没有不舒服,"我哭着说,"她只是很贪睡。如果大家不理她,她可以睡上一整天。要杀了她实在太可怕了。你们不如也杀了我吧!"

在那之后,我就一直牢牢盯着小猫咪,每天晚上我都把她抱到我的床上,让她和我待上很长时间。

但小猫咪的日子并不多了。有一天早晨,我还没起床,妈妈就走进我的房间,坐在我的床边。

"海伦,"她说,"我得告诉你一些会让你感到非常糟糕的事情,但是我希望你能做一个好姑娘,不要让妈妈为此不开心。你知道爸爸和妈妈总是会做他们认为最好的事情的。"

"什么事，妈妈？"我非常害怕，但没有想到是小猫咪的事情。

"你再也见不到你的小猫咪了，"妈妈回答，"她死了。"

"啊，她在哪里？"我哭着问，"她怎么死了？她再也活不过来了吗？"

"是的，"妈妈说，"她是淹死的。"

然后，我便明白是怎么回事了。

"是谁干的？"这是我问出的唯一的话。

"是乔赛亚表哥。"她说，"他费了很多心思，确保小猫一点儿苦都不会受。她立刻就沉到了水底。"

"他是在哪里淹死她的？"

"在磨坊那里，磨坊河谷里，那里的水很深。"妈妈回答说，"是我们告诉他带她去那里的。"

听到这些，我又痛苦地哭了起来。

"我经常跟她去那里玩的，"我嚷道，"只要我活

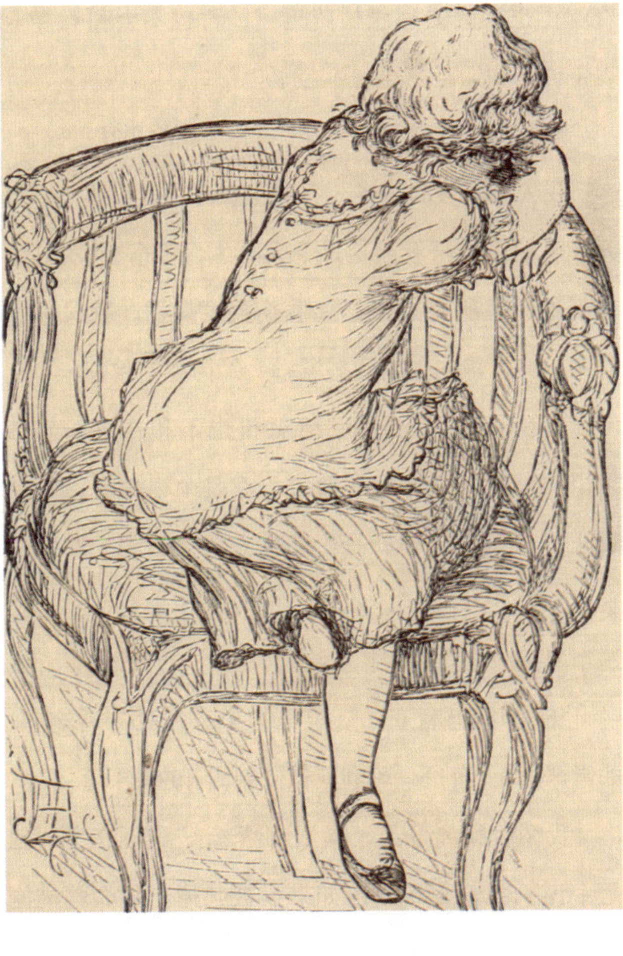

着就再也不会去那座桥附近了,再也不会和乔赛亚表哥讲一句话了,再也不会了!"

妈妈努力安慰我,但是没有用,我的心几乎碎了。

我去吃早饭的时候,乔赛亚表哥也坐在那里,若无其事地读着报纸。他是个大学生,寄宿在我们家。看到他,我所有的愤怒和悲伤再度爆发,我又哭了起来,哭着跑向他,我握紧拳头砸向他的脸。

"我刚刚说只要我活着就再也不和你讲一句话了,"我叫道,"但我还要说,你是个谋杀犯,一个真正的谋杀犯,你就是!等你去做传教士,我希望食人族会把你吃了。我希望他们把你生吞活剥,你这个卑鄙的老谋杀犯!"

"海伦·玛利亚!"爸爸的声音在我身后响起,非常严厉,"海伦·玛利亚!立刻离开这里!"

我绷着脸离开了,嘴里嘟囔着:"我不在乎,他是个谋杀犯。我希望他如果没被吃掉,那么就被淹死好了。圣经里面说了，你们用什么量器量给人，也必用什么量器量给你们。一切皆有报应。他应该被淹死。"

因为这通愤懑的嘟囔，我没有吃到早饭，而早饭之后，我被迫去给乔赛亚表哥道歉。但是我并不是诚心的，一点儿都不是，我只是嘴上说说，重复着别人告诉我的话。从那之后，我尽我所能地不跟他讲话，不正眼看他。

我善良的妈妈提议说再给我一只小猫，但是我不想要了。过了一段日子，我的姐姐安得到了一件礼物，是一只漂亮的灰色小猫，但是我从来都不跟这只小猫玩，也根本不理会她。我对我的小猫咪一片真心，她对我也是。一直到现在，我再也没有养过小猫。

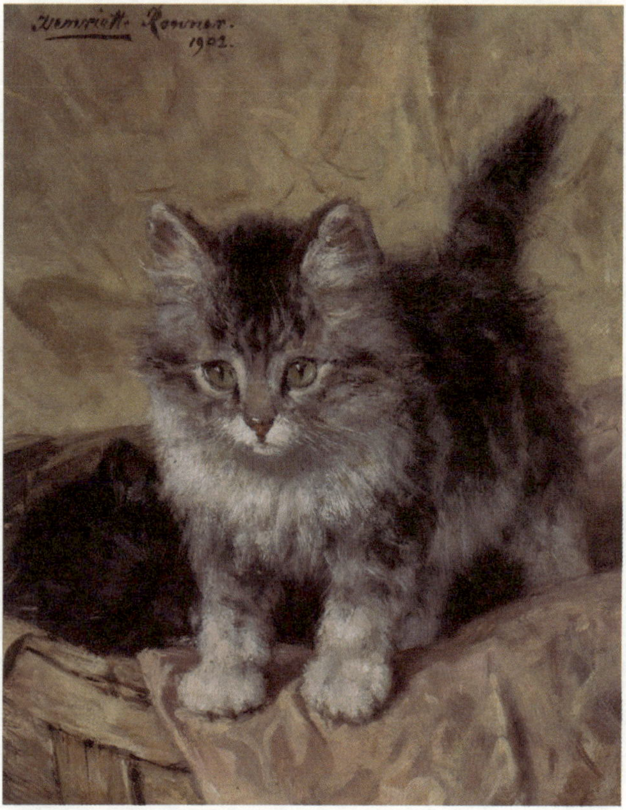
Henriett Ronner.
1902.

# INTRODUCTION

Dear Children,

I do not feel wholly sure that my Pussy wrote these letters herself. They always came inside the letters written to me by my mamma, or other friends, and I never caught Pussy writing at any time when I was at home; but the printing was pretty bad, and they were signed by Pussy's name; and my mamma always looked very mysterious when I asked about them, as if there were some very great secret about it all; so that until I grew to be a big girl, I never doubted but that Pussy printed them all alone by herself, after dark.

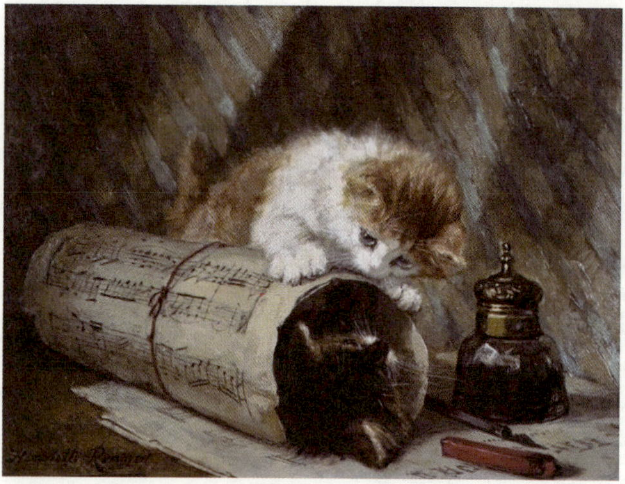

They were written when I was a very little girl, and was away from home with my father on a journey. We made this journey in our own carriage, and it was one of the pleasantest things that ever happened to me. My clothes and my father's were packed in a little leather valise which was hung by straps underneath the carriage, and went swinging, swinging, back and forth, as the wheels went round. My father and I used to walk up all the steep hills, because old Charley, our horse, was not very strong; and I kept my eyes on that valise all the while I was walking behind the carriage; it seemed to me the most unsafe way to carry a valise, and I wished very much that my best dress had been put in a bundle that I could carry in my lap. This was the only drawback on the pleasure of my journey, —my fear that the valise would fall off when we did not know it, and be left in the road, and then I should not have anything nice to wear when I reached my aunt's house. But the valise went through all safe, and I had the satisfaction of wearing my best dress every afternoon while I stayed; and I was foolish enough to think a great deal of this.

On the fourth day after our arrival came a letter from my mamma, giving me a great many directions how to behave, and enclosing this first letter from Pussy. I carried both letters in my apron pocket all the time. They were the first letters I ever had received, and I was very proud of them. I showed them to everybody, and everybody laughed hard at Pussy's, and asked me if I believed that Pussy printed it herself. I thought perhaps my mamma held her paw, with the pen in it, as she had sometimes held my hand for me, and guided my pen to write a few words. I asked papa to please to ask mamma, in his letter, if that were the way Pussy did it; but when his next letter from mamma

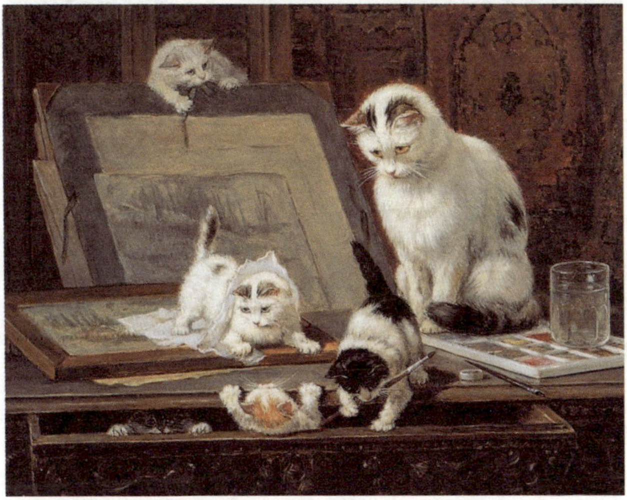

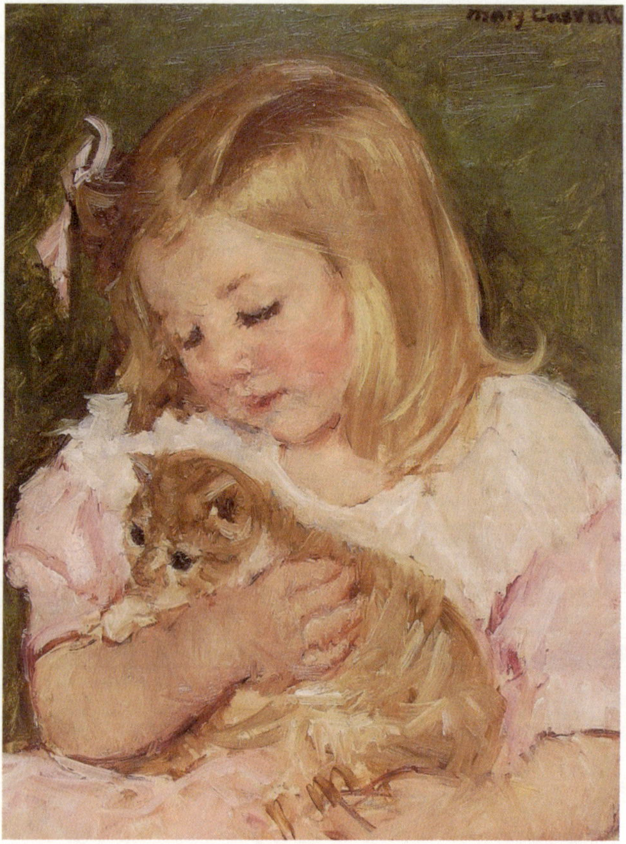

came, he read me this sentence out of it: "Tell Helen I did not hold Pussy's paw to write that letter." So then I felt sure Pussy did it herself; and as I told you, I had grown up to be quite a big girl before I began to doubt it. You see I thought my Pussy such a wonderful Pussy that nothing was too remarkable for her to do. I knew very well that cats generally did not know how to read or write; but I thought there had never been such a cat in the world as this Pussy of mine. It is a great many years since she died; but I can see her before me today as plainly as if it were only yesterday that I had really seen her alive.

She was a little kitten when I first had her; but she grew fast, and was very soon bigger than I wanted her to be. I wanted her to stay little. Her fur was a beautiful dark gray color, and there were black stripes on her sides, like the stripes on a tiger. Her eyes were very big, and her ears unusually long and pointed. This made her look like a fox; and she was so bright and mischievous that some people thought she must be part fox. She used to do one thing that I never heard of any other cat's doing: she used to play hide-and-seek. Did you ever hear of a cat's playing hide-and-seek? And the most wonderful part of it was, that she took it up of her own accord. As soon as she heard me shut the gate in the yard at noon, when school was done, she would run up the stairs as hard as she could go, and take her place at the top, where she could just peep through the banisters. When I opened the door, she would give a funny little mew, something like the mew cats make when they call their kittens. Then as soon as I stepped on the first stair to come up to her, she would race away at the top of her speed, and hide under a bed; and when I reached the room, there would be no Pussy to be seen. If I called her, she would come out

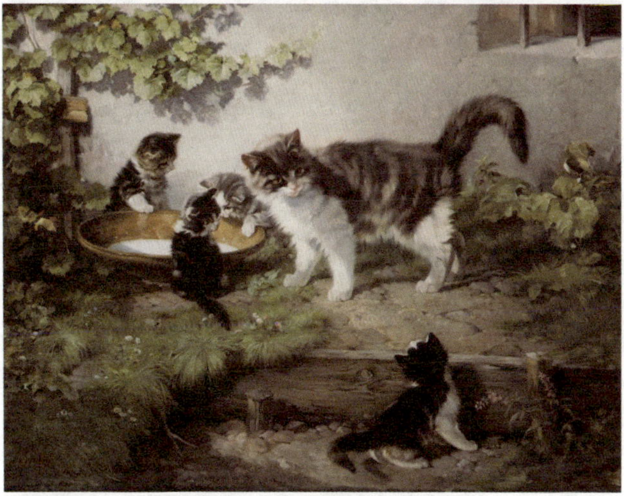

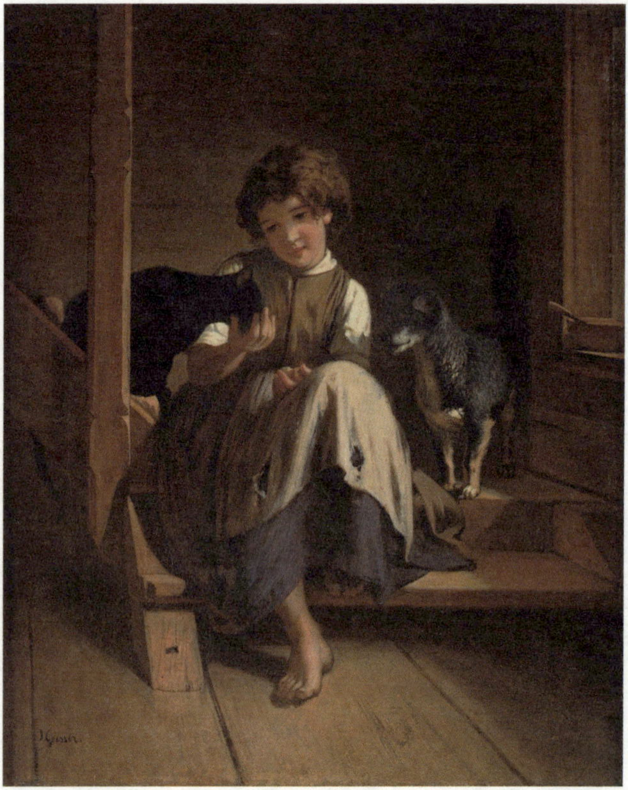

from under the bed; but if I left the room, and went down stairs without speaking, in less than a minute she would fly back to her post at the head of the stairs, and call again with the peculiar mew. As soon as I appeared, off she would run, and hide under the bed as before. Sometimes she would do this three or four times; and it was a favorite amusement of my mother's to exhibit this trick of hers to strangers. It was odd, though; she never would do it twice, when she observed that other people were watching. When I called her, and she came out from under the bed, if there were strangers looking on, she would walk straight to me in the demurest manner, as if it were a pure accident that she happened to be under that bed; and no matter what I did or said, her frolic was over for that day.

She used to follow me, just like a little dog, wherever I went. She followed me to school every day, and we had great difficulty on Sundays to keep her from following us to church. Once she followed me, when it made a good many people laugh, in spite of themselves, on an occasion when it was very improper for them to laugh, and they were all feeling very sad. It was at the funeral of one of the professors in the college.

The professors' families all sat together; and when the time came for them to walk out of the house and get into the carriages to go to the graveyard, they were called, one after the other, by name. When it came to our turn, my father and mother went first, arm-in-arm; then my sister and I; and then, who should rise, very gravely, but my Pussy, who had slipped into the room after me, and had not been noticed in the crowd. With a slow and deliberate gait she walked along, directly behind my sister and me, as if she were the remaining member of the family, as indeed she was. People began to smile, and as we passed through the front door, and went down the steps, some of the men and boys standing there laughed out. I do not wonder; for it must have been a very comical sight. In a second more, somebody sprang forward and snatched Pussy up. Such a scream as she gave! and scratched his face with her claws, so that he was glad to put her down. As soon as I heard her voice I turned round, and called her in a low tone. She ran quickly to me, and I picked her up and carried her in my arms the rest of the way. But I saw even my own papa and mamma laughing a little, for just a minute. That was the only funeral Pussy ever attended.

Pussy lived several years after the events which are related in these letters.

It was a long time before her fur grew out again after that terrible fall into the soft-soap barrel. However, it did grow out at last, and looked as well as ever. Nobody would have known that any thing had been the matter with her, except that her eyes were always weak. The edges of them never got quite well; and poor Pussy used to sit and wash them by the hour; sometimes mewing and looking up in my face, with each stroke of her paw on her eyes, as much as to say, "Don't you see how sore my eyes are? Why don't you do something for me?"

She was never good for any thing as a mouser after that accident, nor for very much to play with. I recollect hearing my mother say one day to somebody, — "Pussy was spoiled by her experience in the cradle. She would like to be rocked the rest of her days, I do believe; and it is too funny to see her turn up her nose at tough beef. It was a pity she ever got a taste of tenderloin!"

At last, what with good feeding and very little exercise,

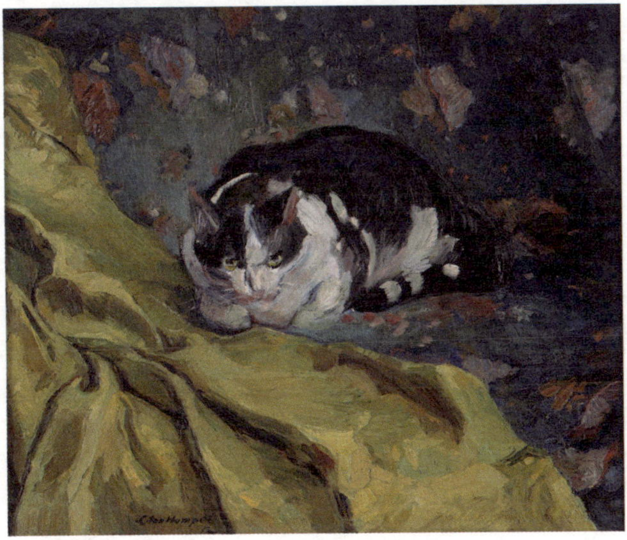

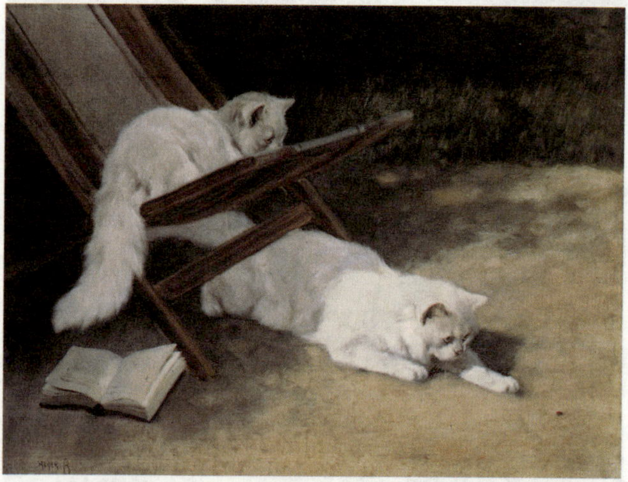

she grew so fat that she was clumsy, and so lazy that she did not want to do any thing but lie curled up on a soft cushion.

She had outgrown my little chair, which had a green moreen cushion in it, on which she had slept for many a year, and of which I myself had very little use, —she was in it so much of the time. But now that this was too tight for her, she took possession of the most comfortable places she could find, all over the house. Now it was a sofa, now it was an arm-chair, now it was the foot of somebody's bed. But wherever it happened to be, it was sure to be the precise place where she was in the way, and the poor thing was tipped headlong out of chairs, shoved hastily off sofas, and driven off beds so continually, that at last she came to understand that when she saw any person approaching the chair, sofa, or bed on which she happened to be lying, the part of wisdom for her was to move away. And it was very droll to see the injured and reproachful expression with which she would slowly get up, stretch all her legs, and walk away, looking for her next sleeping-place. Everybody in the house, except me, hated the sight of her; and I had many a pitched battle with the servants in her behalf. Even my mother, who was the kindest human being I ever knew, got out of patience at last, and said to me one day: —

"Helen, your Pussy has grown so old and so fat, she is no comfort to herself, and a great torment to everybody else. I think it would be a mercy to kill her."

"Kill my Pussy!" I exclaimed, and burst out crying, so loud and so hard that I think my mother was frightened; for she said quickly: —

"Never mind, dear; it shall not be done, unless it is necessary. You would not want Pussy to live, if she were very uncomfortable all the time."

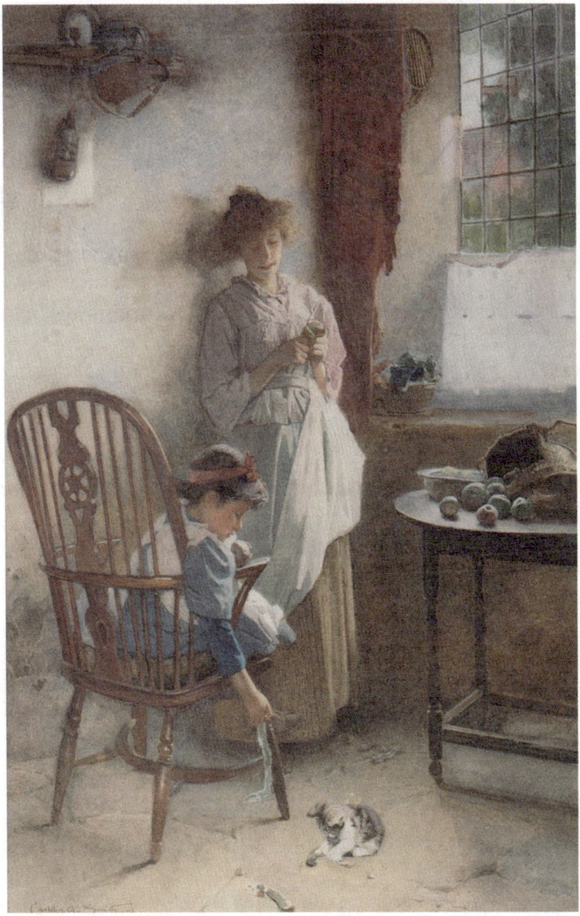

"She isn't uncomfortable," I cried; "she is only sleepy. If people would let her alone, she would sleep all day. It would be awful to kill her. You might as well kill me!"

After that, I kept a very close eye on Pussy; and I carried her up to bed with me every night for a long time.

But Pussy's days were numbered. One morning, before I was up, my mamma came into my room, and sat down on the edge of my bed.

"Helen," she said, "I have something to tell you which will make you feel very badly; but I hope you will be a good little girl, and not make mamma unhappy about it. You know your papa and mamma always do what they think is the very best thing."

"What is it, mamma?" I asked, feeling very much frightened, but never thinking of Pussy.

"You will never see your Pussy any more," she replied.

"She is dead."

"Oh, where is she?" I cried. "What killed her? Won't she come to life again?"

"No," said my mother; "she is drowned."

Then I knew what had happened.

"Who did it?" was all I said.

"Cousin Josiah," she replied; "and he took great care that Pussy did not suffer at all. She sank to the bottom instantly."

"Where did he drown her?" I asked.

"Down by the mill, in Mill Valley, where the water is very deep," answered my mother; "we told him to take her there."

At these words I cried bitterly.

"That's the very place I used to go with her to play," I exclaimed. "I'll never go near that bridge as long as I live, and I'll never speak a word to Cousin Josiah

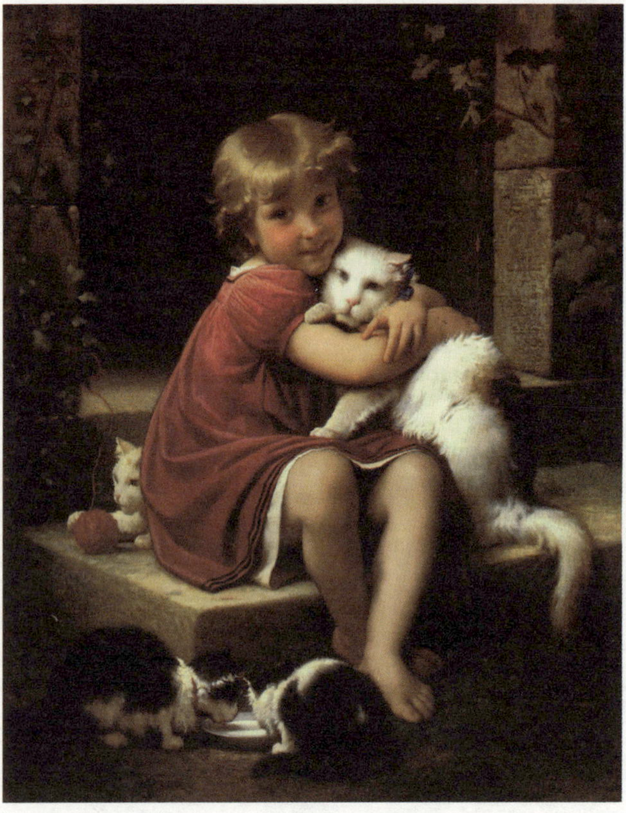

either—never!"

My mother tried to comfort me, but it was of no use; my heart was nearly broken.

When I went to breakfast, there sat my cousin Josiah, looking as unconcerned as possible, reading a newspaper. He was a student in the college, and boarded at our house. At the sight of him all my indignation and grief broke forth afresh. I began to cry again; and running up to him, I doubled up my fist and shook it in his face.

"I said I'd never speak to you as long as I lived," I cried; "but I will. You're just a murderer, a real murderer; that's what you are! and when you go to be a missionary, I hope the cannibals'll eat you! I hope they'll eat you alive raw, you mean old murderer!"

"Helen Maria!" said my father's voice behind me, sternly. "Helen Maria! leave the room this moment!"

I went away sullenly, muttering, "I don't care, he is a murderer; and I hope he'll be drowned, if he isn't eaten! The Bible says the same measure ye mete shall be meted to you again. He ought to be drowned."

For this sullen muttering I had to go without my breakfast; and after breakfast was over, I was made to beg Cousin Josiah's pardon; but I did not beg it in my heart—not a bit—only with my lips, just repeating the words I was told to say; and from that time I never spoke one word to him, nor looked at him, if I could help it.

My kind mother offered to get another kitten for me, but I did not want one. After a while, my sister Ann had a present of a pretty little gray kitten; but I never played with it, nor took any notice of it at all. I was as true to my Pussy as she was to me; and from that day to this, I have never had another Pussy!

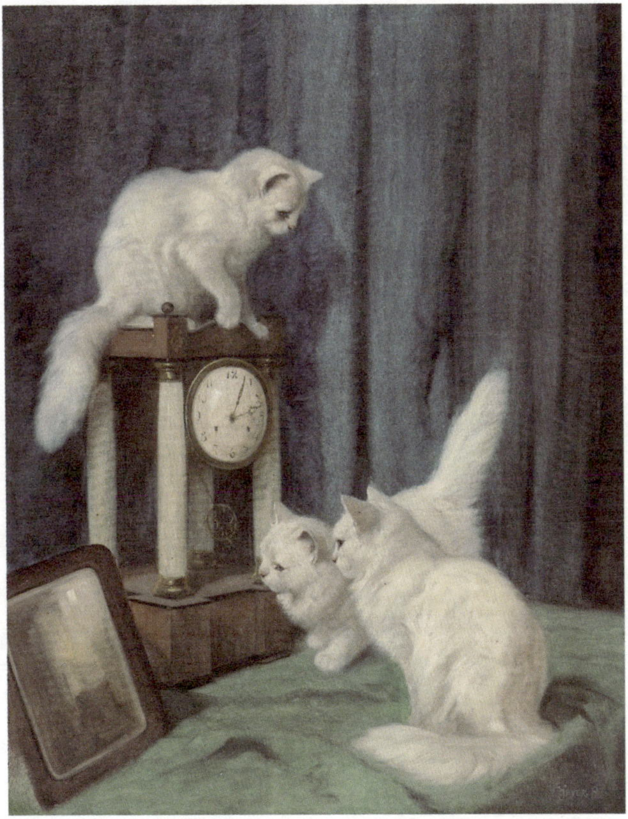

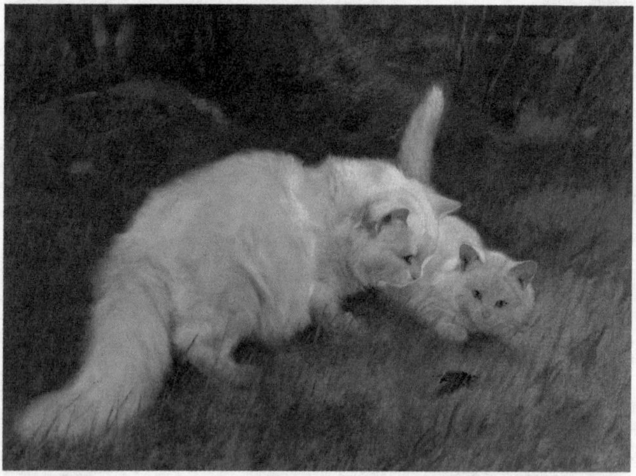

## 第一封信

我亲爱的海伦：

你妈妈是这么叫你的，我知道。因为我跳到了写字桌上，看到了她给你的信。——她现在不在房间里。我肯定我也有权和她一样这么叫你，因为如果你是我自己生的小猫，长得和我一样，那我对你的爱也不会比现在更多。我在你的大腿上睡过多少好觉啊！你从自己的饭中给我省下了多少美味的肉啊！啊，只要我活着，就不会让任何一只老鼠染指你的任何一样东西。

从你昨天出发之后，我就觉得不开心，完全不知道我一只猫该做什么。我去了谷仓，觉得可以在干草垛上睡一觉，因为我认为，对于不开心的人来说，

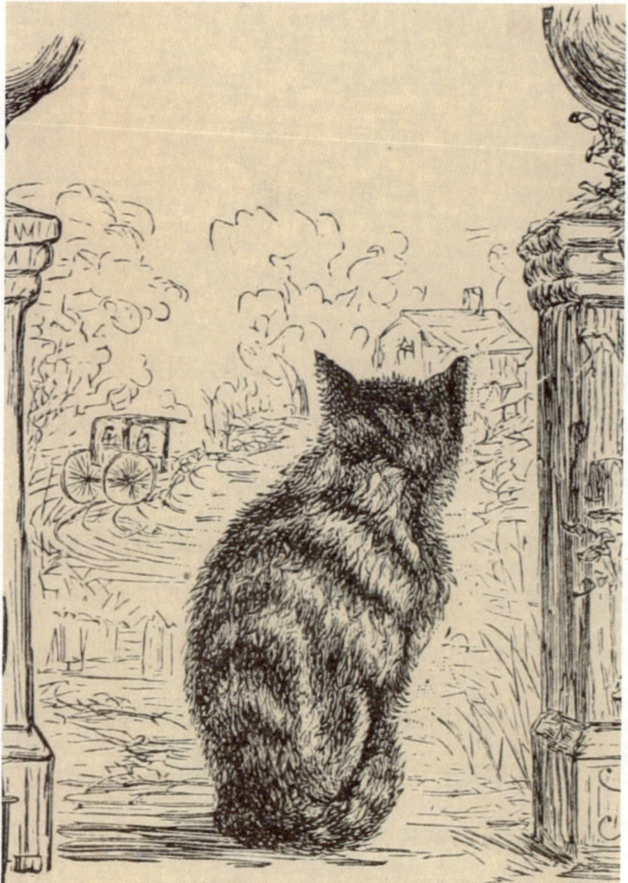

睡觉是最好的事情；但是老查雷没有在他的畜栏里跺脚踏步，我觉得实在太孤单了，真是受不了。于是我便去了花园，躺在大马士革玫瑰丛下面抓苍蝇玩。有一种苍蝇绕着花丛飞来飞去，它的味道比我吃过的任何一种苍蝇都好吃。你应该明白，我抓苍蝇和你抓苍蝇是存在很大的不同的。我注意过，你从来都不吃它们，我真好奇，为什么你总是对我这么好，却又会残忍地毫无缘由地屠杀可怜的苍蝇。我经常希望能有机会和你谈谈这件事。既然你亲爱的妈妈已经教会了我如何写字，那么我就可以跟你讲很多我过去无法让你理解的事情——我过去总是为此不开心。因为学不会英语，我非常沮丧，我觉得也没有人会费力气学习猫语，所以我们猫族就被局限住了，只能和别的猫交流，不然我们就能知道更多的东西。而且，安默斯特只有几只猫，我在这里非常孤独，如果没有希区柯克太太的猫和迪金森先生的

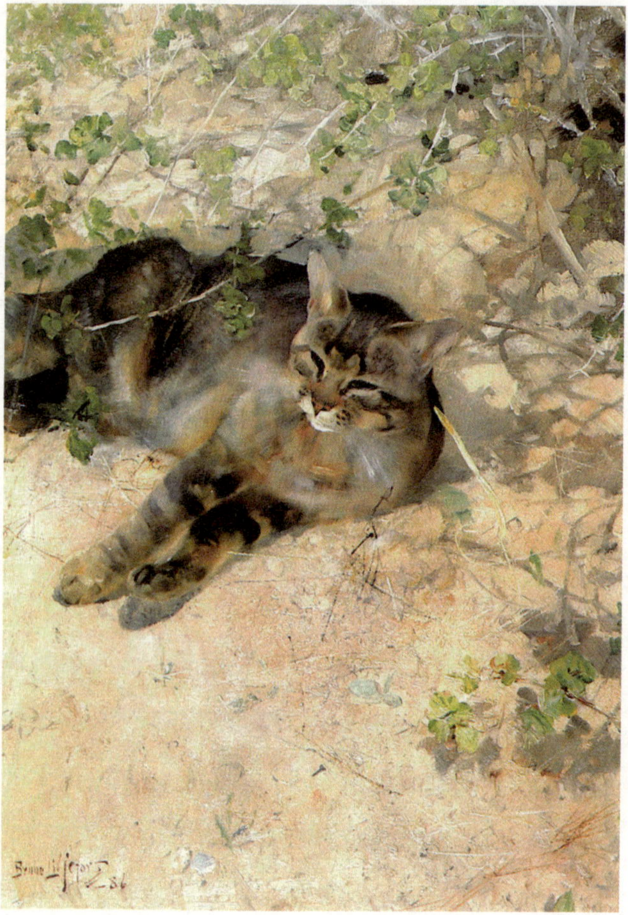

猫，我应该已经忘了怎么说话了。你在家的时候，我一点儿都不在意，尽管我不能跟你说话，但是我能懂得你对我说的每一个字。我们一起玩红球玩得多开心啊。那个红球现在被收在了起居室的小缝纫桌底层的抽屉中。你妈妈把它放进去的时候，扭头对我说："可怜的小猫，海伦回家之前，你没有什么好玩的了。"我觉得我应该大哭一场，但我转念一想，如果哭了也无济于事，再哭的话就十分愚蠢了，所以我假装左眼里面进了东西，抬起爪子揉眼睛。我很少为了什么事情哭泣，除非是为了打翻的牛奶。我必须得承认，我经常为了打翻的牛奶哭泣，而猫的牛奶总是被打翻。人们总是把给猫的牛奶放在又旧又破的容器里，随便一碰就会翻，然后又会把这装了奶的容器放到肯定会碍事的地方。有很多次，我那放在猫舍里的蓝色碟子都被乔赛亚给打翻了。你以为我吃了丰盛美味的牛奶早餐，可实际上我什么都没有吃到，只有

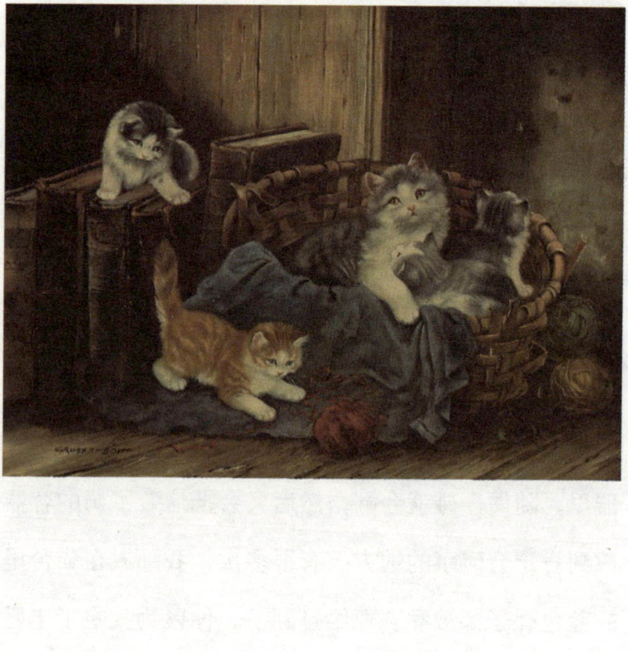

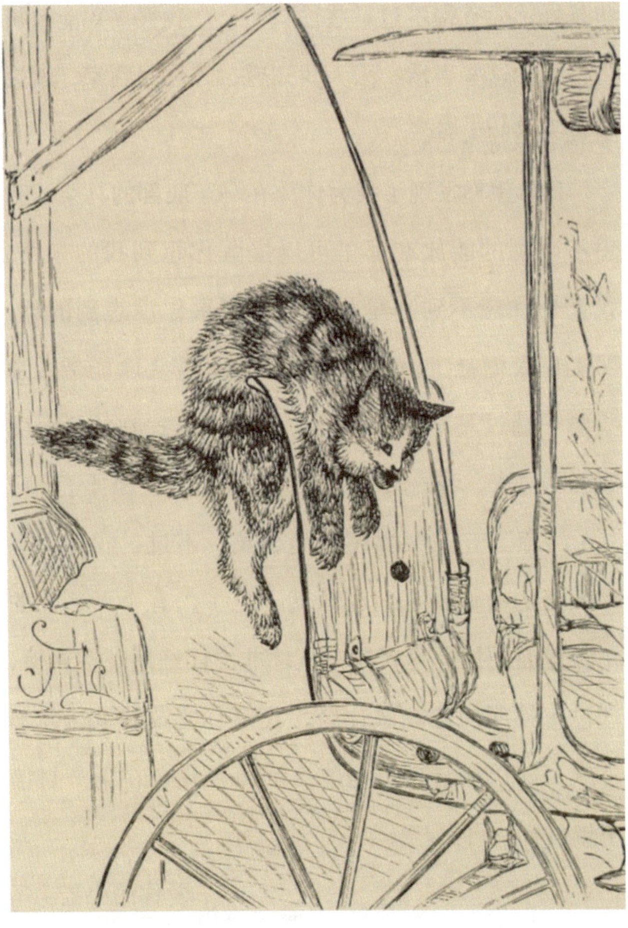

些苍蝇，而苍蝇不过是些佐料而已。我很高兴能有机会告诉你这些事情，因为我知道，等你回到家，就会给我丰盛的大餐。

我希望你发现了我为你放在马车底部的马栗。我想不出别的能放在那里可以提醒你想到我的东西。我害怕你想不到那是我放的，如果你没想到的话，那实在太糟糕了，因为我吃了不少苦头才能带着那些栗子翻过马车的挡泥板，为了把能找到的最大的栗子叼过去，我一直大张着嘴，下巴都快僵掉了。

门廊上有三朵漂亮的蒲公英，不过，我觉得到你回家的时候，它们应该就不见了。有个人来你的花园里面鼓捣，尽管我一直都非常仔细地观察着他，却没有搞明白他在做什么。我担心他做的事情你不喜欢，如果搞清楚了是怎么回事，我会在下一封信中告诉你。再见。

*爱你的小猫*

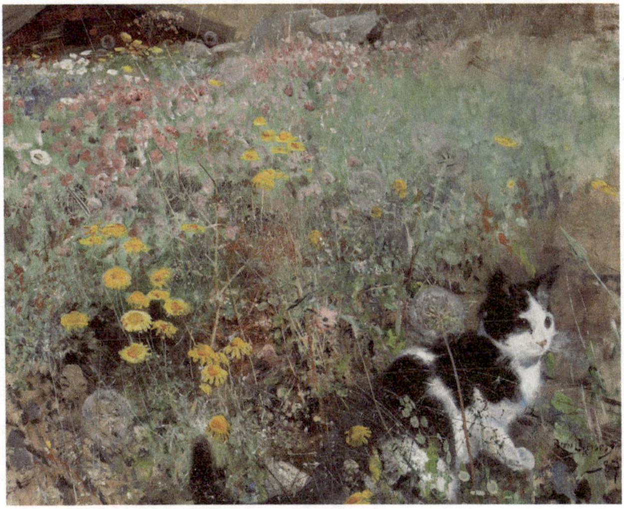

I

My Dear Helen,

That is what your mother calls you, I know, for I jumped up on writing table just now, and looked, while she was out of the room; and I am sure I have as much right to call you so as she has, for if you were my own little kitty, and looked just like me, I could not love you any more than I do. How many good naps I have had in your lap! And how many nice bits of meat you have saved for me out of your own dinner! Oh, I'll never let a rat, or a mouse, touch any thing of yours so long as I live.

I felt very unhappy after you drove off yesterday, and

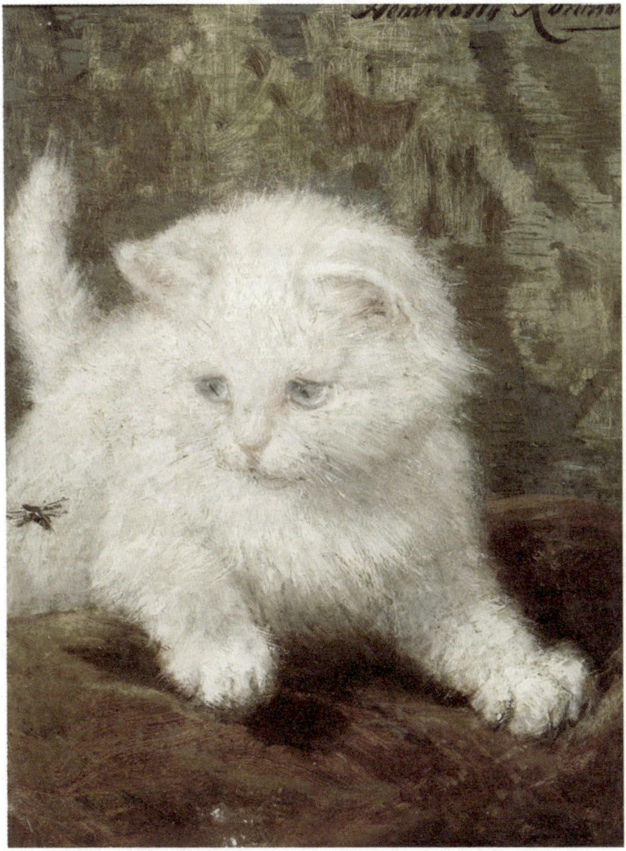

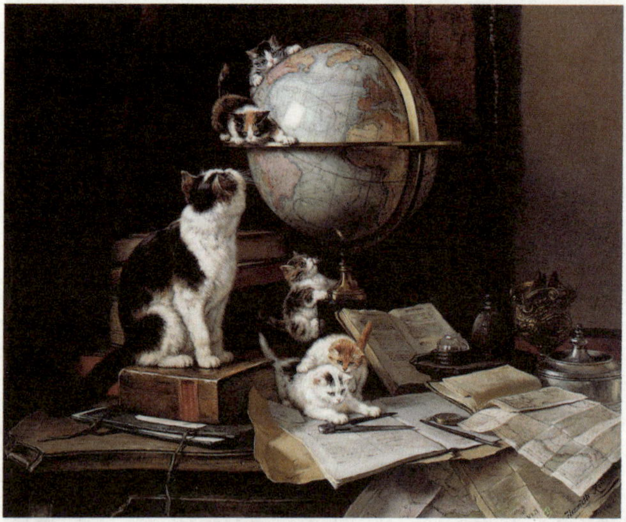

did not know what to do with myself. I went into the barn, and thought I would take a nap on the hay, for I do think going to sleep is one of the very best things for people who are unhappy; but it seemed so lonely without old Charlie stamping in his stall that I could not bear it, so I went into the garden, and lay down under the damask rose bush, and caught flies. There is a kind of fly round that bush which I like better than any other I ever ate. You ought to see that there is a very great difference between my catching flies and your doing it. I have noticed that you never eat them, and I have wondered that when you were always so kind to me you could be so cruel as to kill poor flies for nothing. I have often wished that I could speak to you about it: now that your dear mother has taught me to print, I shall be able to say a great many things to you which I have often been unhappy about because I could not make you understand. I am entirely discouraged about learning to speak the English language, and I do not think anybody takes much trouble to learn ours; so we cats are confined entirely to the society of each other, which prevents our knowing so much as we might; and it is very lonely too, in a place where there are so few cats kept as in Amherst. If it were not for Mrs. Hitchcock's cat, and Judge Dickinson's, I should really forget how to use my tongue. When you are at home I do not mind it, for although I cannot talk to you, I understand every word that you say to me, and we have such good plays together with the red ball. That is put away now in the bottom drawer of the little workstand in the sitting-room. When your mother put it in, she turned round to me, and said, "Poor pussy, no more good plays for you till Helen comes home!" and I thought I should certainly cry. But I think it is very foolish to cry over what cannot be helped,

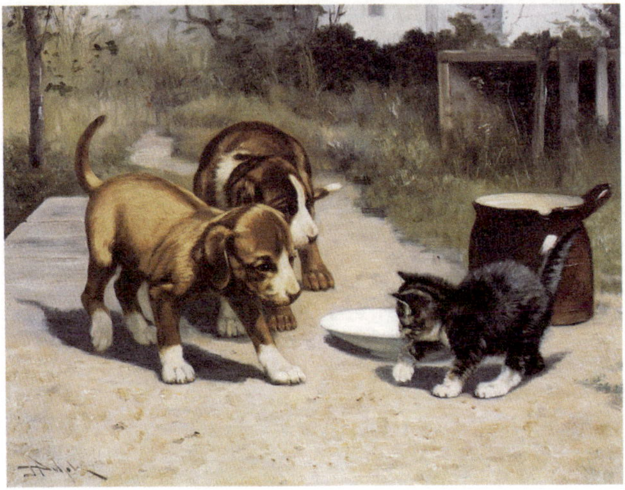

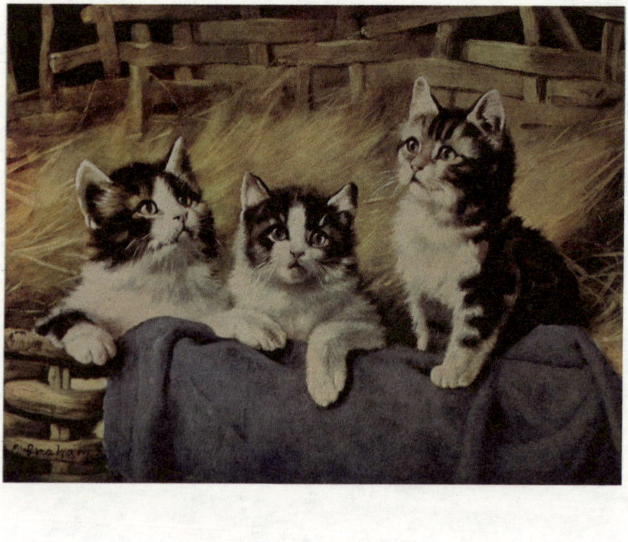

so I pretended to have got something into my left eye, and rubbed it with my paw. It is very seldom that I cry over any thing, unless it is "spilt milk". I must confess, I have often cried when that has happened: and it always is happening to cats' milk. They put it into old broken things that tip over at the least knock, and then they set them just where they are sure to be most in the way. Many's the time Josiah has knocked over that blue saucer of mine, in the shed, and when you have thought that I had had a nice breakfast of milk, I had nothing in the world but flies, which are not good for much more than just a little sort of relish. I am so glad of a chance to tell you about this, because I know when you come home you will get a better dish for me.

I hope you found the horse chestnuts which I put in the bottom of the carriage for you. I could not think of any thing else to put in, which would remind you of me: but I am afraid you will never think that it was I who put them there, and it will be too bad if you don't, for I had a dreadful time climbing up over the dasher with them, and both my jaws are quite lame from stretching them so, to carry the biggest ones I could find.

There are three beautiful dandelions out on the terrace, but I don't suppose they will keep till you come home. A man has been doing something to your garden, but though I watched him very closely all the time, I could not make out what he was about. I am afraid it is something you will not like; but if I find out more about it, I will tell you in my next letter. Good bye.

Your affectionate Pussy.

## 第二封信

我亲爱的海伦：

我希望你和你爸爸能马上回来，无论你现在在哪里，只要你接到这封信，就尽快回家来。如果你没有尽快回来，那么当你回到家的时候，就已经没有家了。我非常害怕，非常紧张，我的爪子一直抖，把墨水瓶弄翻了两次，洒了很多墨水出来，现在墨水瓶中的墨水所剩无多，而且底部的这些像是麦粉布丁一样浓稠，所以，这封信的样子不好，你必须谅解，我会尽快把这里发生的可怕的事情告诉你。

就在昨天，我写完上一封信还不到一个小时，我听到客厅中传来一声很大的声响，便跑去看到底是

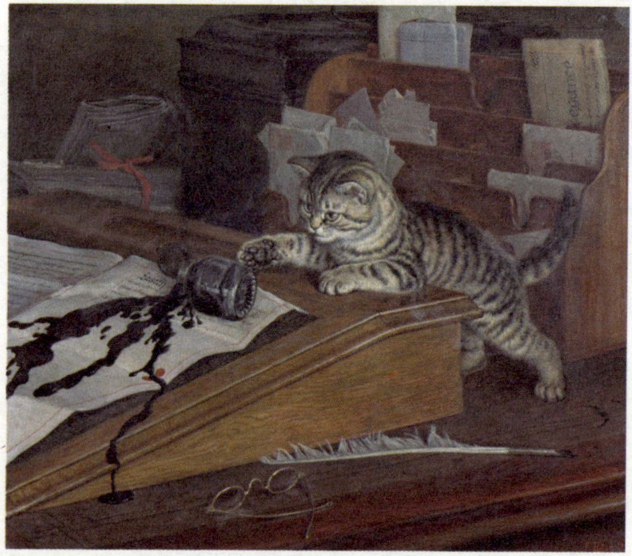

怎么回事。玛丽正在那里，头上扎着她最糟糕的一条蓝手帕，身上穿着她洗衣日时穿的罩袍，手里拿着一把大锤子。她一看到我，就说："就是那只猫！总是碍我的事！"说着她就拿起一个小凳子砸向我，然后砰的一声关上了客厅的门。所以，我跑出去了，到前窗下面听着，因为我肯定她在做着什么不想让别人知道的坏事。我过去从来都没有听过那样的声音：所有东西都被移动了。几分钟之后，你知道发生了什么吗？整个地毯砸到了我头上！我几乎被灰尘给呛死了，而且我身体内的所有骨头似乎都被砸断了，但是我努力从毯子下面爬了出来。然后，我听到玛丽说："真希望不再受那只猫折腾！我真希望好心的海伦能把她带走。"这时，我无比肯定，她必然在筹划些坏事。于是我便跑到了花园里，爬上了台阶底部的苹果树，顺着一根树枝尽量往外爬，从那里我能够直接透过客厅的窗户看进去。天啊！我亲爱的海伦,你能想象我当时的感觉吗?我看到所有的桌子、椅子,还有书架都堆在房间中央的地板上,书都被装在了大篮子里。玛丽用她最快的速度把窗户一扇一扇地卸下来。我忘了告诉你了,昨天晚上你妈妈出去了。我觉得她是去哈德利了。在我看来,极有可能,玛丽是想在你妈妈回来之前,把所有能移动的东西都带上逃跑。过了一会儿,那个住在斯雷特家的爱尔兰丑女人到了咱们家后门。你知道我说的是谁,就是那个去年春天向我泼冷水的人。看到她过来,我十分肯定,她和玛丽要趁你们都不在家联手将我杀掉,所以我从树上跳下来,匆忙之间弄裂了我最好的那只爪子。然后我跑去了面包师的果林,那天剩下的时间,我都躲在那里,饥寒交迫,十分凄惨。一些低洼处还有积雪,我的脚湿了,感觉非常难受。除了一只干瘪瘦弱的老鼹鼠以外,我没有找到任何食物。春天的鼹鼠一向都不好吃。说

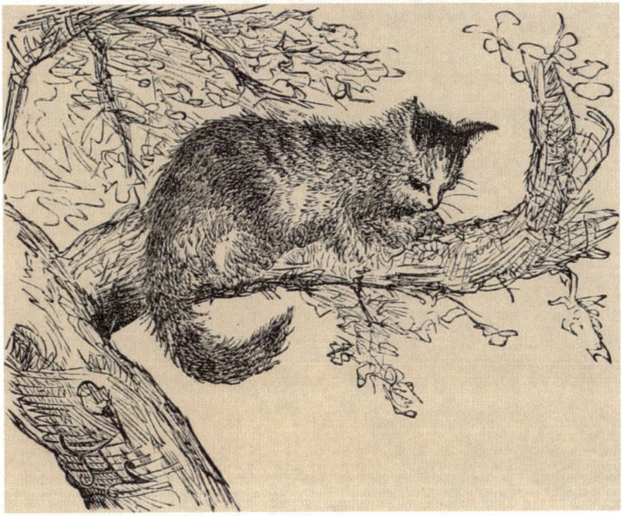

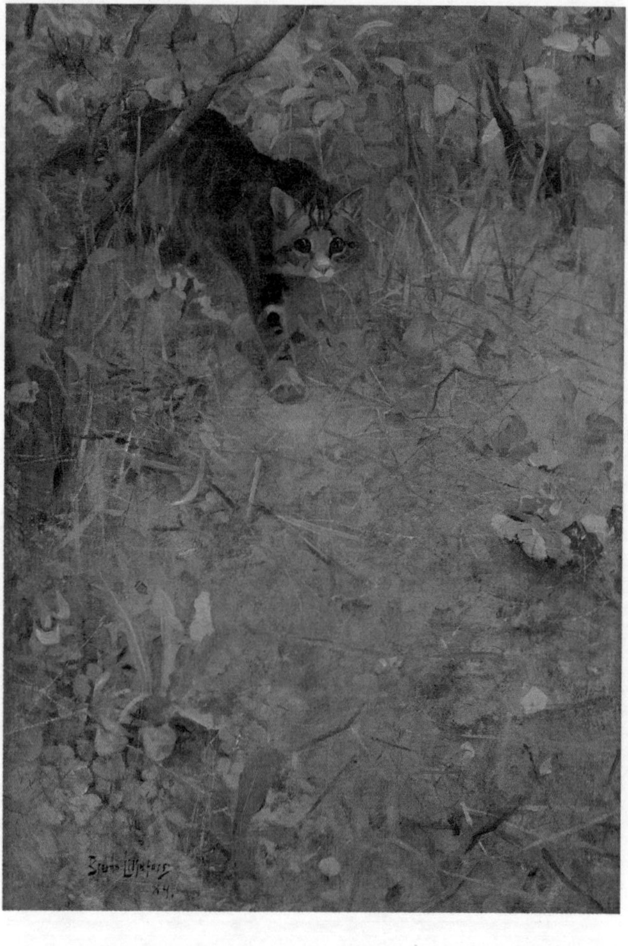

实话，没有人了解我们猫过的是多么凄惨的生活，哪怕是我们当中最幸运的猫，生活也是凄惨的！

天黑之后，我回了家，但是玛丽把所有门都锁上了，甚至是后面小屋的那扇小门。所以，我不得不跳到了地下室里，自从那次我跳到地下室落在牛奶盘子边缘造成了肩膀严重扭伤，我就再也不愿意跳入地下室了。我偷偷爬到厨房楼梯的顶上，像老鼠一样蹑手蹑脚，就仿佛我是个惯窃。我在那里聆听了很长时间，玛丽正和那个爱尔兰女人说话，我努力想搞清楚她们在筹划什么。但是我一直都听不懂爱尔兰话，我一直听着，因为一动不动待了太久，四条腿都抽筋了，可我还是没有听明白。甚至玛丽说的事情，我也听不懂，通常情况下，我是能很轻松地听懂她的话的。我在一个装胡萝卜的箱子里过了一夜，非常非常不舒服。

今天早晨，一听到玛丽走下通向地下室的台阶，我便藏到了拱门里。趁她在撇去牛奶浮沫的时候，我溜到了楼上，跑进了起居室里。里面的一切都混乱不堪，地毯不见了，窗户也不见了，我觉得有些椅子也被搬走了。所有的瓷器都装在大篮子里，放在了餐具室的地面上。你父母的衣服都被从育儿室的壁橱里面取了出来，放在椅子上。看着这所有的一切，我只能干站着，什么都做不了，这感觉真的很糟糕。我觉得，在这之前，我从来都没有完全明白身为一只猫有什么劣势。我穿过街道，把这些事情讲给了法官的猫听。她年纪很大，很傻，一心只想着她的六只小猫（那些是我见过的最丑的小猫了），完全都不关心她邻居的事情。希区柯克太太今天早晨从你家经过，我跑出去找她，咬住她的裙子拉扯，用尽了我所有的办法，想让她进屋，但她说："不了，不了，小猫，我今天不进去了，你的女主人不在。"我得说，我都哭出来了。我坐在路中间，一动不动

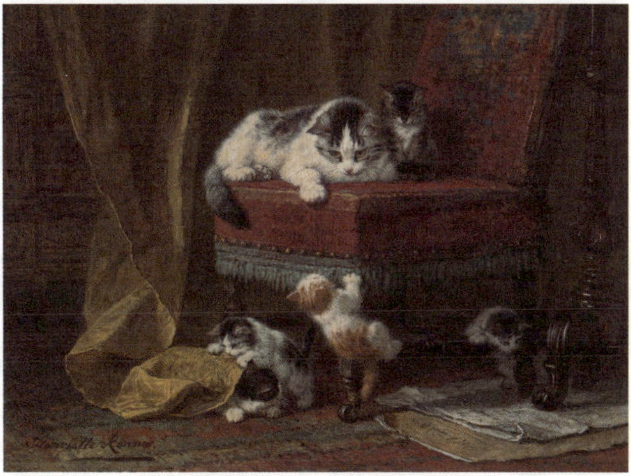

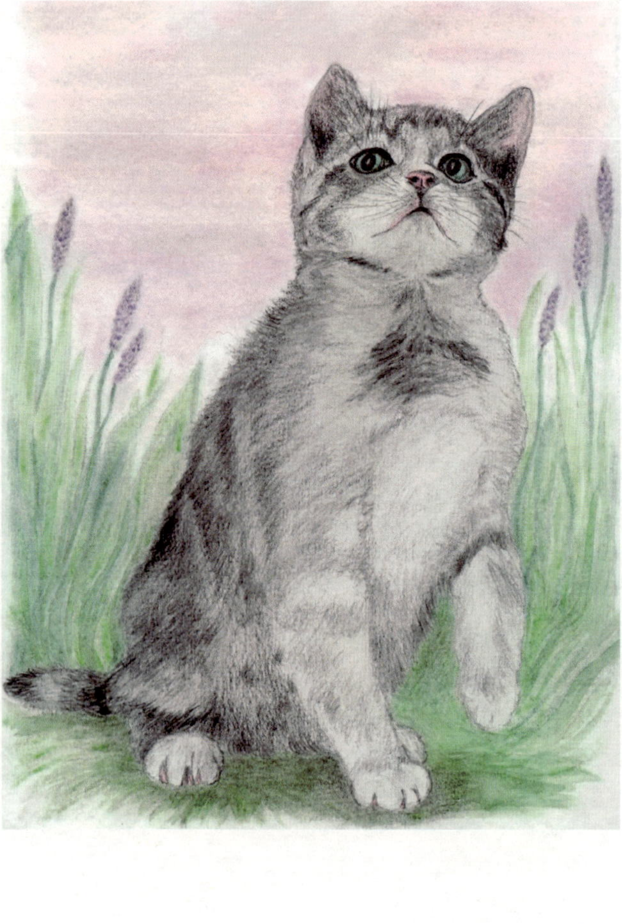

地待了半个小时。

昨天，我听说你的朋友汉娜·多伦斯要给你写信，所以，我现在正跑着上山，把我的信带去给她。我觉得当她看到我的时候肯定会大吃一惊，因为我非常肯定镇上别的猫都不会写字。请尽快回家来。

爱你的小猫

附：就在刚才，两个男人赶着车到了前门，他们正在把所有的地毯都装到车上去。噢，天啊，噢，天啊，真希望我知道自己该做些什么！还有，我刚听到玛丽对他们说："请尽快，因为我想要在人们回来之前处理完这事。"

## II

My Dear Helen,

I do wish that you and your father would turn around directly, wherever you are, when you get this letter, and come home as fast as you can. If you do not come soon there will be no home left for you to come into. I am so frightened and excited, that my paws tremble, and I have upset the ink twice, and spilled so much that there is only a little left in the bottom of the cup, and it is as thick as hasty pudding; so you must excuse the looks of this letter, and I will tell you as quickly as I can about the dreadful state of things here.

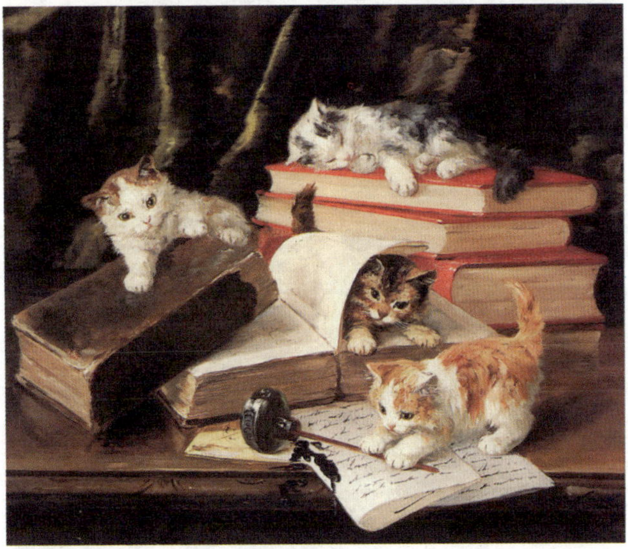

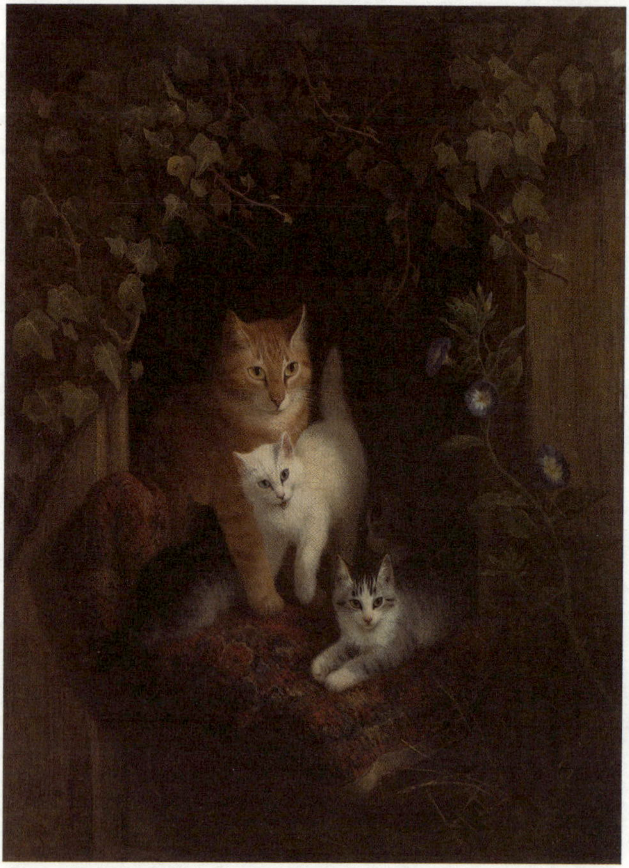

Not more than an hour after I finished my letter to you, yesterday, I heard a great noise in the parlor, and ran in to see what was the matter. There was Mary with her worst blue handkerchief tied over her head, her washing-day gown on, and a big hammer in her hand. As soon as she saw me, she said, "There's that cat! Always in my way," and threw a cricket at me, and then shut the parlor door with a great slam. So I ran out and listened under the front windows, for I felt sure she was in some bad business she did not want to have known. Such a noise I never heard: all the things were being moved; and in a few minutes, what do you think—out came the whole carpet right on my head! I was nearly stifled with dust, and felt as if every bone in my body must be broken; but I managed to creep out from under it, and heard Mary say, "If there isn't that torment of a cat again! I wish to goodness Helen had taken her along!" Then I felt surer than ever that some mischief was on foot: and ran out into the garden, and climbed up the old apple-tree at the foot of the steps, and crawled out on a branch, from which I could look directly into the parlor windows. Oh! my dear Helen, you can fancy how I felt, to see all the chairs and tables and bookshelves in a pile in the middle of the floor, the books all packed in big baskets, and Mary taking out window after window as fast as she could. I forgot to tell you that your mother went away last night. I think she has gone to Hadley to make a visit, and it looks to me very much as if Mary meant to run away with every thing which could be moved, before she comes back. After a while that ugly Irishwoman, who lives in Mr. Slater's house, came into the back gate: you know the one I mean, —the one that threw cold water on me last spring. When I saw her coming I felt sure that she

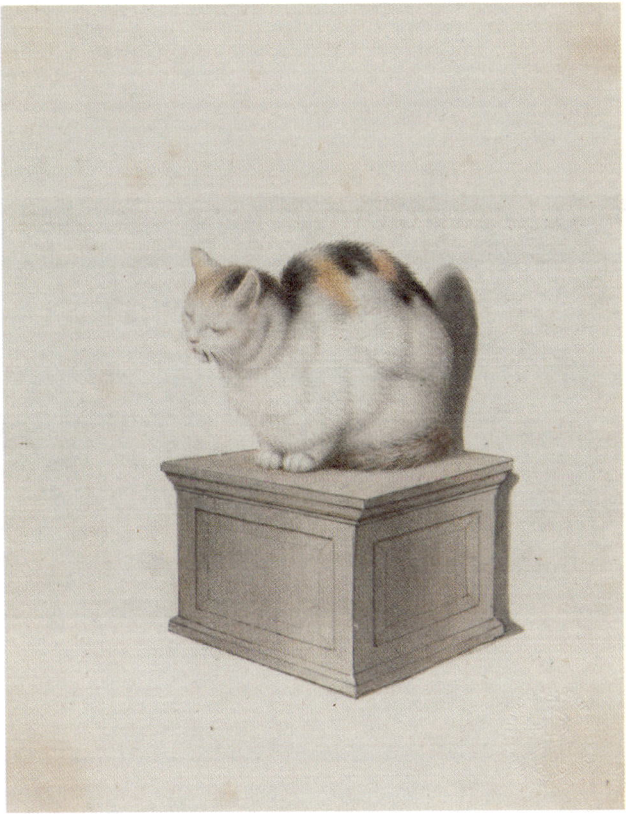

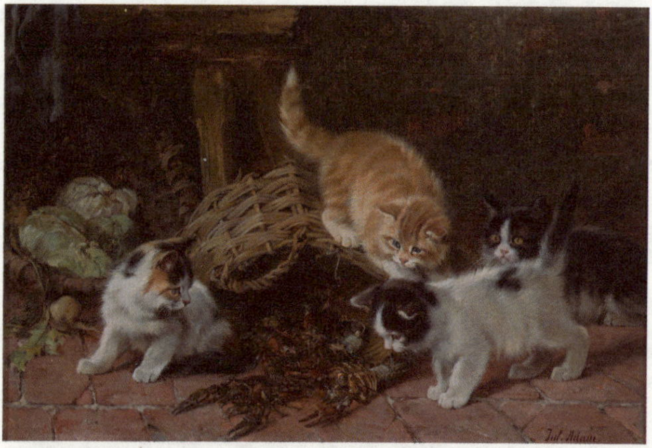

and Mary meant to kill me, while you were all away; so I jumped down out of the tree, and split my best claw in my hurry, and ran off into Baker's Grove, and stayed there all the rest of the day, in dreadful misery from cold and hunger. There was some snow in the hollows, and I wet my feet, which always makes me feel wretchedly; and I could not find any thing to eat except a thin dried-up old mole. They are never good in the spring. Really, nobody does know what hard lives we cats lead, even the luckiest of us!

After dark, I went home; but Mary had fastened up every door, even the little one into the back shed. So I had to jump into the cellar window, which is a thing I never like to do since I got that bad sprain in my shoulder from coming down on the edge of a milk pan. I crept up to the head of the kitchen stairs, as still as a mouse, if I'm any judge, and listened there for a long time, to try and makeout, from Mary's talk with the Irishwoman, what they were planning to do. But I never could understand Irish, and although I listened till I had cramps in all my legs, from being so long in one position, I was no wiser. Even the things Mary said I could not understand, and I usually understand her very easily. I passed a very uncomfortable night in the carrot bin.

As soon as I heard Mary coming down the cellar stairs, this morning, I hid in the arch, and while she was skimming the milk, I slipped upstairs, and ran into the sitting-room. Every thing there is in the same confusion; the carpet is gone; and the windows too, and I think some of the chairs have been carried away. All the china is in great baskets on the pantry floor; and your father and mother's clothes are all taken out of the nursery closet, and laid on chairs. It is very dreadful to have to stand

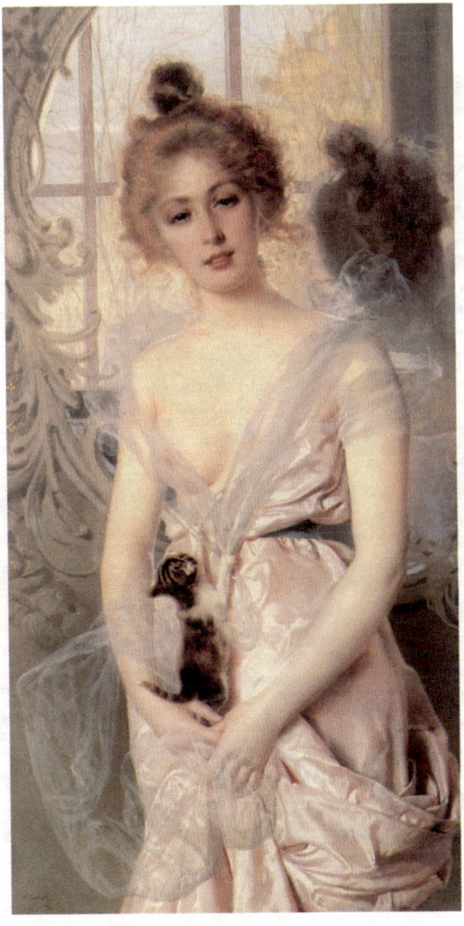

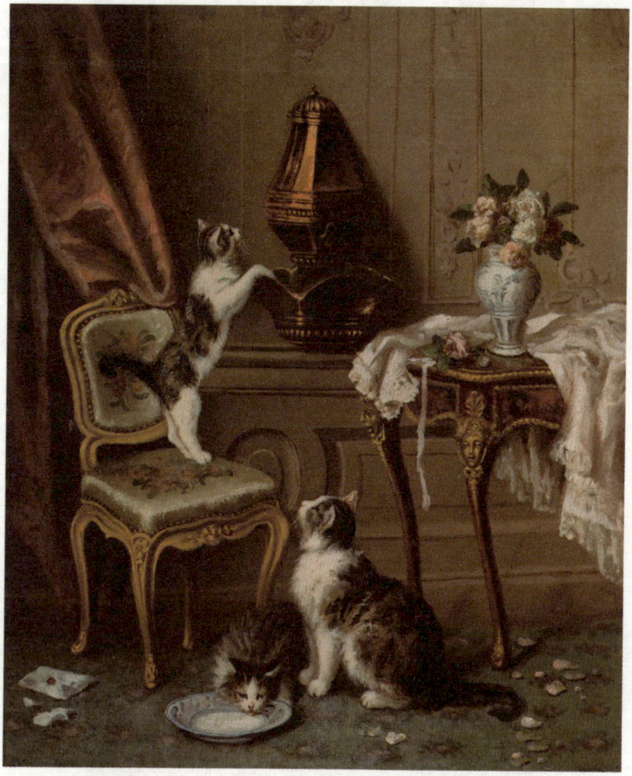

and see all this, and not be able to do any thing. I don't think I ever fully realized before the disadvantage of being only a cat. I have just been across the street, and talked it all over with the Judge's cat, but she is very old and stupid, and so taken up with her six kittens (who are the ugliest I ever saw), that she does not take the least interest in her neighbors' affairs. Mrs. Hitchcock walked by the house this morning, and I ran out to her, and took her dress in my teeth and pulled it, and did all I could to make her come in, but she said, "No, no, pussy, I'm not coming in today; your mistress is not at home." I declare I could have cried. I sat down in the middle of the path, and never stirred for half an hour.

I heard your friend, Hannah Dorrance, say yesterday, that she was going to write to you today, so I shall run up the hill now and carry my letter to her. I think she will be astonished when she sees me, for I am very sure that no other cat in town knows how to write. Do come home as soon as possible.

> Your affectionate Pussy.

P. S. Two men have just driven up to the front gate in a great cart, and they are putting all the carpets into it. Oh dear, oh dear, if I only knew what to do! And I just heard Mary say to them, "Be as quick as you can, for I want to get through with this business before the folks come back."

## 第三封信

我亲爱的海伦：

我摔得很惨，浑身僵硬酸疼，再也不能多写一行字，但是我必须告诉你，我之前那么恐慌是非常愚蠢的，为此我很尴尬。房子和东西都很安全，你妈妈已经回来了。等我拿起钢笔不那么痛的时候，就把一切都写下来告诉你。

纳尔逊家的房子搬来了新人，我觉得他们是很和气的人，因为他们把牛奶装在黄色的陶盘里。他们还带来了一只漂亮的黑猫，他叫恺撒。所有人都在谈论他，他的胡须是我见过的最帅的。我真希望自已能尽快好起来,能快点儿见到他,无论如何,我不想他看到现在的我。

        爱你的小猫

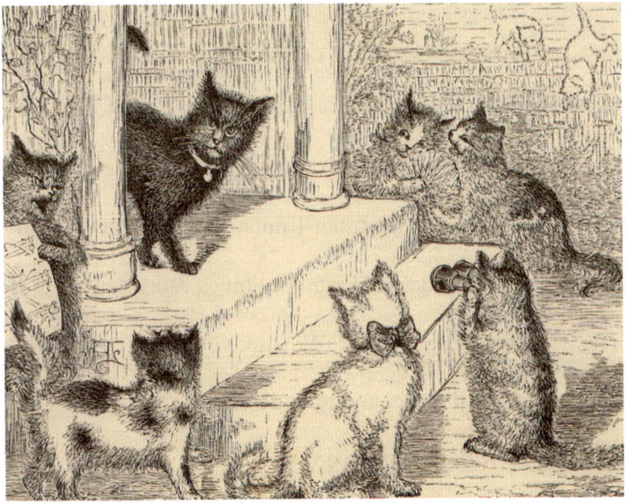

## III

My Dear Helen,

I am too stiff and sore from a terrible fall I have had, to write more than one line; but I must let you know that my fright was very silly, and I am very much mortified about it. The house and the things are all safe; your mother has come home; and I will write, and tell you all, just as soon as I can use my pen without great pain.

Some new people have come to live in the Nelson house; very nice people, I think, for they keep their milk in yellow crockery pans. They have brought with them a splendid black cat whose name is Caesar, and everybody

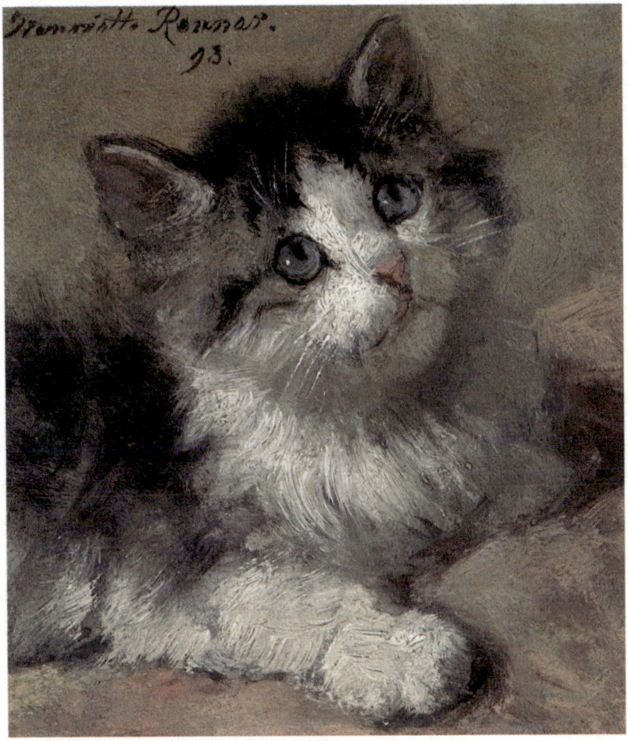
93.

is talking about him. He has the handsomest whiskers I ever saw. I do hope I shall be well enough to see him before long, but I wouldn't have him see me now for any thing.

                                          Your affectionate Pussy.

## 第四封信

我亲爱的海伦：

有一件事情，猫和男人或是女人都一样不喜欢，就是自己出丑。我上次给你写那封长信，告诉你玛丽把所有的家具都搬了出去、要把房子拆了的事情，实在是出了一个天大的丑。要把最后的结果告诉你，我真的感觉非常羞愧，但是我知道你非常爱我，会因为我平白经历了这么一场糟糕的恐慌而可怜我。

我给你写完上次那封信之后的三天中，情况每况愈下。你妈妈没有回家来，那个可怕的爱尔兰女人却一直在这里。我不敢靠近房子，我必须告诉你，我都快饿死了。我一般都卧在玫瑰花丛下面，尽我所能地观察事情的动向，偶尔才去谷仓中抓一只老鼠。但是那种重口味的食物我已经吃不惯了，因为自从和你一起生活以来，我就开始习惯了清淡的饮食。第三天，我身体虚弱，难受得动弹不得，所以一整天都躺在查雷的畜栏的草堆里。饥饿和焦虑之中，我真的觉得我要死了。中午的时候，我听到玛丽在小屋里面说："我相信那只讨厌的猫已经自己跑了，不管怎么样说真是让人开心。但我还是想知道那个烦人精到底怎么了！"

我浑身发抖，我知道，如果她来到谷仓，她那沉重的脚随便一踢，就会要了我的命。而我太虚弱了，根本跑不掉。到了傍晚，我听到你亲爱的妈妈的声音，她呼唤道："可怜的小猫，哎呀，可怜的小猫，你跑哪儿去了？"

我经常听到有人说猫是没有感情的，但是亲爱的海伦，你得相信，那些人全都大错特错了。如果他

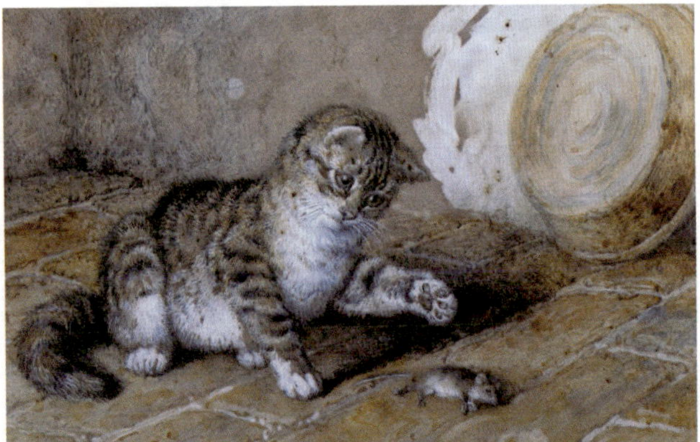

们了解我在那个时候的感觉,他们肯定会改变看法的。我高兴坏了,都叫不出声了。我的脚似乎被牢牢地粘在地上了,我没有办法走到你妈妈跟前。她把我抱在怀里,带着我穿过厨房,来到了起居室。玛丽正在厨房里面煎蛋糕,你妈妈经过灶台边时,用她最甜美的声音说:"你看我找到可怜的小猫了,玛丽。"

"唔,"玛丽说,"我还真没想到,她想被人找到的时候原来能这么快就被发现。"

我知道这是谎言,因为我听到她在小屋说的话了。我真希望搞明白到底为什么她这么讨厌我,我也希望她能知道我有多讨厌她。我真的要考虑趁哪天晚上去把她的袜子和鞋子都咬烂。而这也不过是和她扯平而已。她绝对不会怀疑到我的,因为她的房间里面有很多老鼠。只要我觉得是她柜子里的老鼠,我就不去抓。

起居室里面的一切都井然有序——一种光滑的白色的东西，样子有些像是篮子的侧面，铺满了地板，壁炉上面盖着粉白相间的漂亮的纸帘子，窗户上挂着白色平纹布窗帘。我一动不动地在屋子中间站了很长一段时间，被惊得呆在了那里。天啊，真希望我能够说话，能告诉你妈妈发生的事情，告诉她三天前屋子里是个什么样子。这时，你妈妈说："可怜的小猫，我知道你都快饿死了，是不是？"我回答："是啊！"不过，只是一声喵而已。然后，她给我拿来了一个装满了浓奶油的大汤碗，里面还掺了一些最最美味的冷肉丁。我从来都没有吃过这么好吃的东西。我把东西吃光之后，你妈妈抱起我，把我放在她的大腿上，说："可怜的小猫，我们很想小海伦，是不是？"她一直把我放在腿上，直到睡觉时间。她还让我睡在她的床尾，这是我这辈子最快乐的夜晚之一。半夜的时候，我醒来了一会儿，

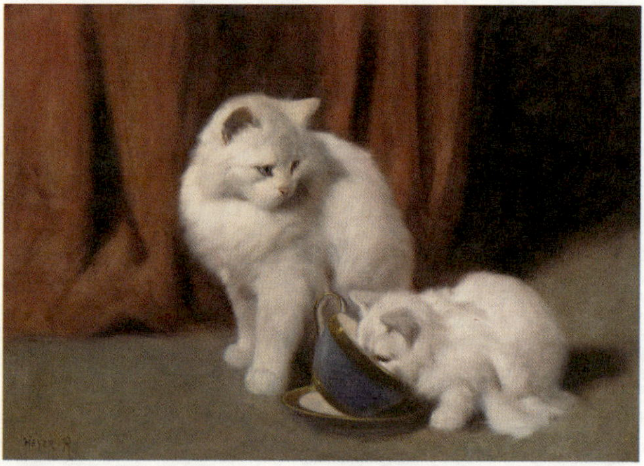

抓到了一只刚出窝的小老鼠,我第一次见到那么小的老鼠。这样的小老鼠肉很嫩。

早上,我和你妈妈在餐厅吃早餐,餐厅和起居室一样漂亮。早餐之后,希区柯克太太来了,你妈妈说:"想想就觉得我很幸运啊,玛丽趁我外出把整个房子大扫除了一番。每个房间都干净整洁,所有羊毛衣服都整理出去了,给夏衣腾出了地方。可怜的小猫,被吓得跑到了外面,我估计,要是我们在家,肯定也会被吓得跑出去。"

你能想象我有多羞愧吗?我跑到桌子底下,一直到希区柯克太太走了之后才出来。不过,接下来才是故事最伤心的部分。我从桌下出来不久,就透过窗户看到外面,发现在樱桃树下的地上有我这辈子见过的最肥的最诱人的知更鸟。窗户看上去像是没有玻璃一样,我想当然地认为是被取下来放到了楼上,柴架、地毯都是这样的,等到冬天再拿下楼来。

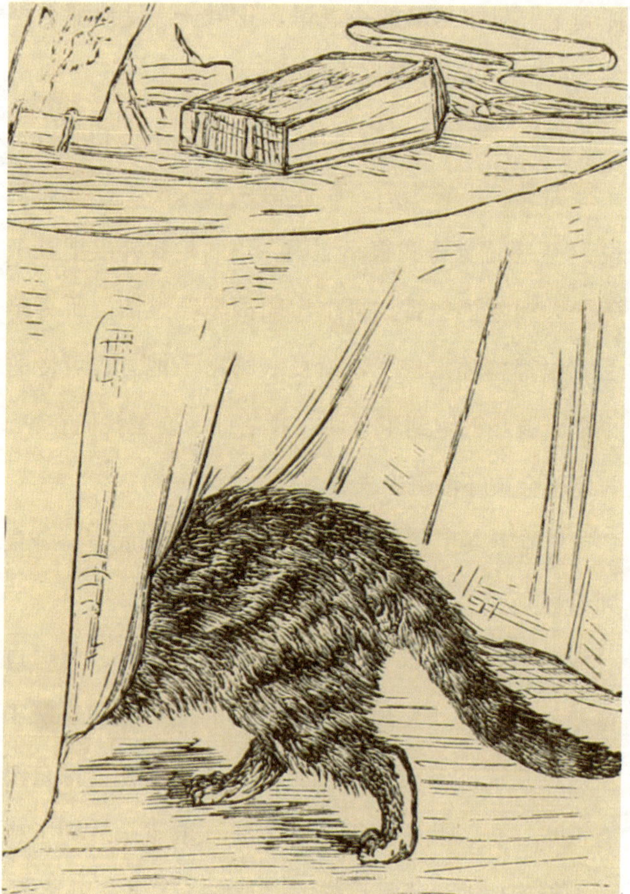

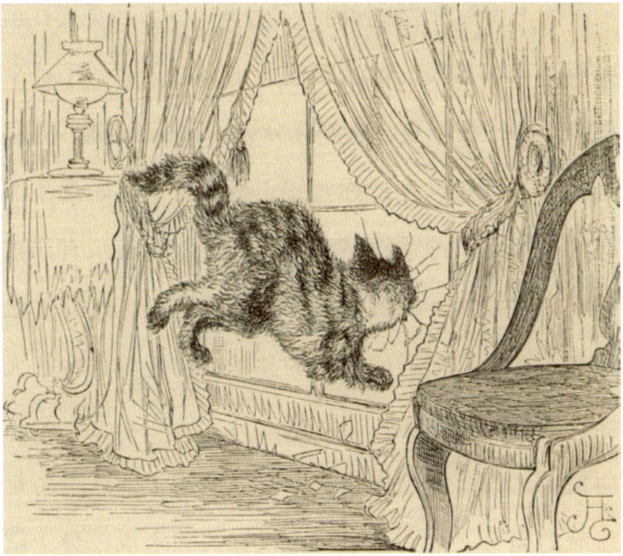

我知道如果我想要抓住那只知更鸟，就一点儿时间都不能浪费，所以我就用尽全力，猛地跳了过去。噢，我亲爱的海伦，我相信你绝对没听过那么大的一声撞击：我几乎被弹回到了房间中间，我觉得我至少滚了六圈。我的鼻血喷涌而出，右耳撞到了一个桌脚上，受伤严重，有好几分钟，我什么都听不到。当我缓过神来，发现你妈妈正抱着我，用她那条漂亮的手帕蘸了冷水擦拭我的脸。我的右前爪有严重的瘀伤，很疼，搞得我没有办法洗脸，也没有办法写字。情况最糟糕的是我的鼻子。凡是看到我的人都笑话我，我不怪他们，我的鼻子看起来有原来的两倍大，我非常担忧它不会复原如初了。这可将是致命的痛苦，谁不知道对一只猫的脸来说，鼻子就是美丑的关键呢？每一个到家里来的人都会听到我摔下来的故事，我自己都已经听烦了。那些人听了之后全都笑得喘不过来气，特别是我还没来得及躲到桌子底下被他们看到了我的鼻子的时候。

如果不是因为这些,我本该早点儿给你写信的,也会写得更长些,但是我的爪子疼得厉害,我的一只眼睛因为鼻子的肿胀几乎睁不开,所以,我必须就此搁笔了。

      爱你的小猫

附:我上封信中跟你说过恺撒吧?当然,我不想在目前这种状况下出门,所以我只从窗口看到过他。

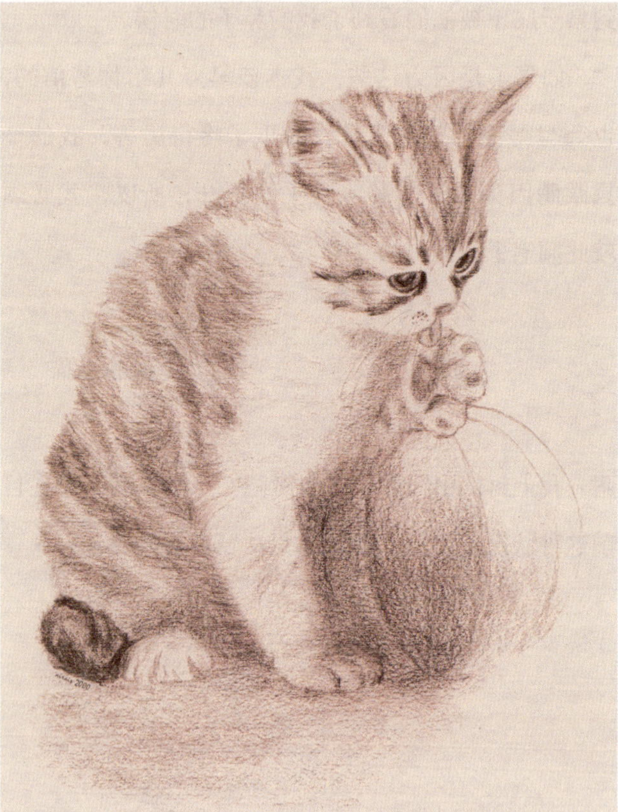

## IV

My Dear Helen,

There is one thing that cats don't like any better than men and women do, and that is to make fools of themselves. But a precious fool I made of myself when I wrote you that long letter about Mary's moving out all the furniture, and taking the house down. It is very mortifying to have to tell you how it all turned out, but I know you love me enough to be sorry that I should have had such a terrible fright for nothing.

It went on from bad to worse for three more days after I wrote you. Your mother did not come home; and the awful Irishwoman was here all the time. I did not dare to go near the house, and I do assure you I nearly starved: I used to lie under the rose-bushes, and watch as well as I could what was going on: now and then I caught a rat in the barn, but that sort of hearty food never has agreed with me since I came to live with you, and became accustomed to a lighter diet. By the third day I felt too weak and sick to stir: so I lay still all day on the straw in Charlie's stall; and I really thought, between the hunger and the anxiety, that I should die. About noon I heard Mary say in the shed, "I do believe that everlasting cat has taken herself off: it's a good riddance anyhow, but I should like to know what has become of the plaguy thing!"

I trembled all over, for if she had come into the barn I know one kick from her heavy foot would have killed me, and I was quite too weak to run away. Towards night I heard

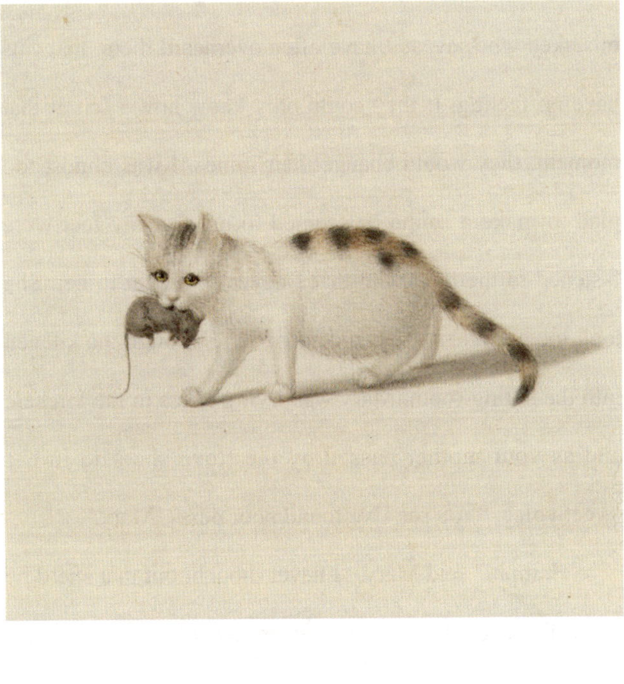

your dear mother's voice calling, "Poor pussy, why, poor pussy, where are you?"

I assure you, my dear Helen, people are very much mistaken who say, as I have often overheard them, that cats have no feeling. If they could only know how I felt at that moment, they would change their minds. I was almost too glad to make a sound. It seemed to me that my feet were fastened to the floor, and that I never could get to her. She took me up in her arms, and carried me through the kitchen into the sitting-room. Mary was frying cakes in the kitchen, and as your mother passed by the stove she said in her sweet voice, "You see I've found poor pussy, Mary."

"Humph," said Mary, "I never thought but that she'd be found fast enough when she wanted to be!"

I knew that this was a lie, because I had heard what she said in the shed. I do wish I knew what makes her hate

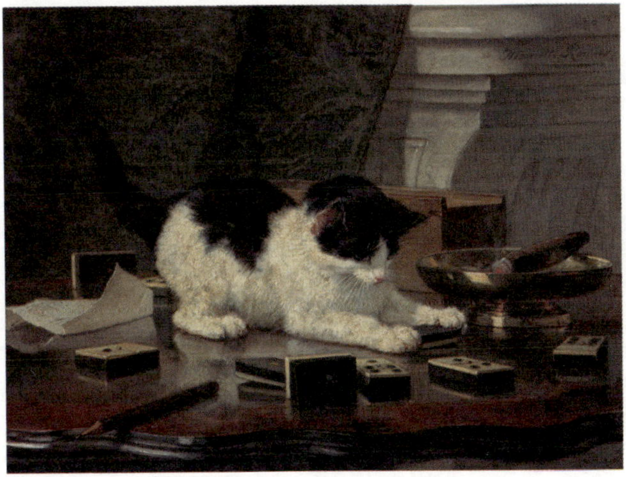

me so: I only wish she knew how I hate her. I really think I shall gnaw her stockings and shoes some night. It would not be any more than fair; and she would never suspect me, there are so many mice in her room, for I never touch one that I think belongs in her closet.

The sitting-room was all in most beautiful order, —a smooth white something, like the side of a basket, over the whole floor, a beautiful paper curtain, pink and white, over the fire-place, and white muslin curtains at the windows. I stood perfectly still in the middle of the room for some time. I was too surprised to stir. Oh, how I wished that I could speak, and tell your dear mother all that had happened, and how the room had looked three days before. Presently she said, "Poor pussy, I know you are almost starved, aren't you?" and I said "Yes." as plainly as I could mew it. Then she brought me a big soup-plate full of thick cream, and

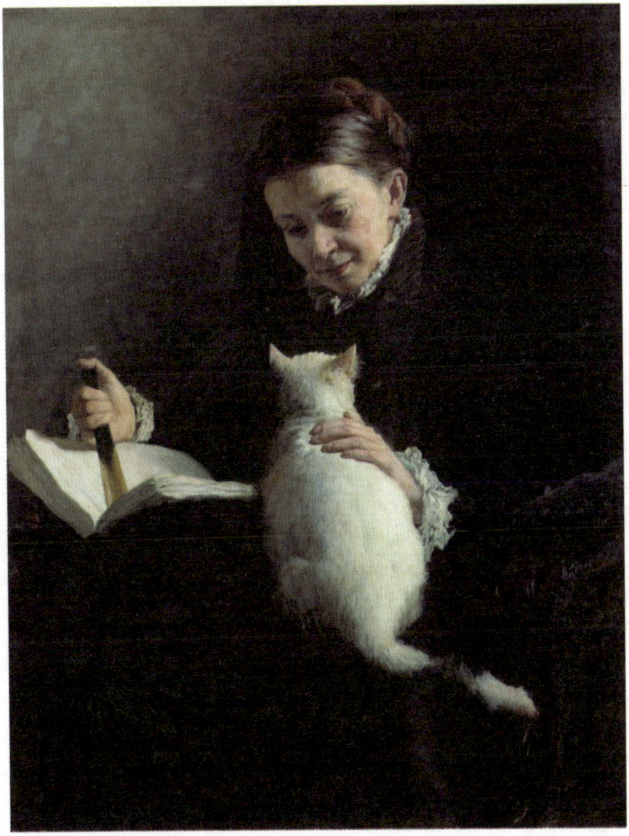

some of the most delicious cold hash I ever tasted; and after I had eaten it all, she took me in her lap, and said, "Poor pussy, we miss little Helen, don't we?" and she held me in her lap till bed-time. Then she let me sleep on the foot of her bed: it was one of the happiest nights of my life. In the middle of the night I was up for a while, and caught the smallest mouse I ever saw out of the nest. Such little ones are very tender.

In the morning I had my breakfast with her in the dining-room, which looks just as nice as the sitting-room. After breakfast Mrs. Hitchcock came in, and your mother said: "Only think, how fortunate I am; Mary did all the house-cleaning while I was away. Every room is in perfect order; all the woollen clothes are put away for the summer. Poor pussy, here, was frightened out of the house, and I suppose we should all have been if we had been at home."

Can you imagine how ashamed I felt? I ran under the table and did not come out again until after Mrs. Hitchcock had gone. But now comes the saddest part of my story. Soon after this, as I was looking out of the window, I saw the fattest, most tempting robin on the ground under the cherry-tree: the windows did not look as if they had any glass in them, and I took it for granted that it had all been taken out and put away upstairs, with the andirons and the carpets, for next winter. I knew that there was no time to be lost if I meant to catch that robin, so I ran with all my might and tried to jump through. Oh, my dear Helen, I do not believe you ever had such a bump: I fell back nearly into the middle of the room; and it seemed to me that I turned completely over at least six times. The blood streamed out of my nose, and I cut my right ear very

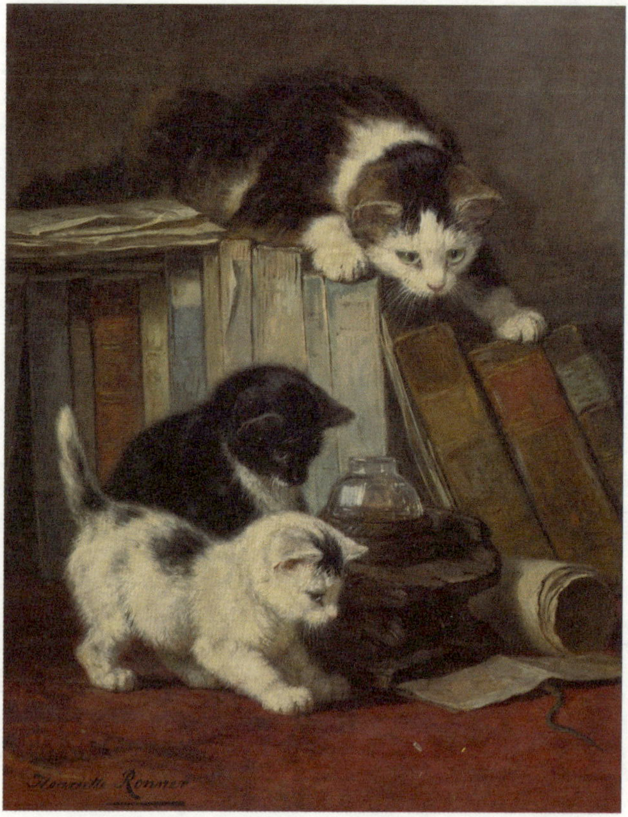

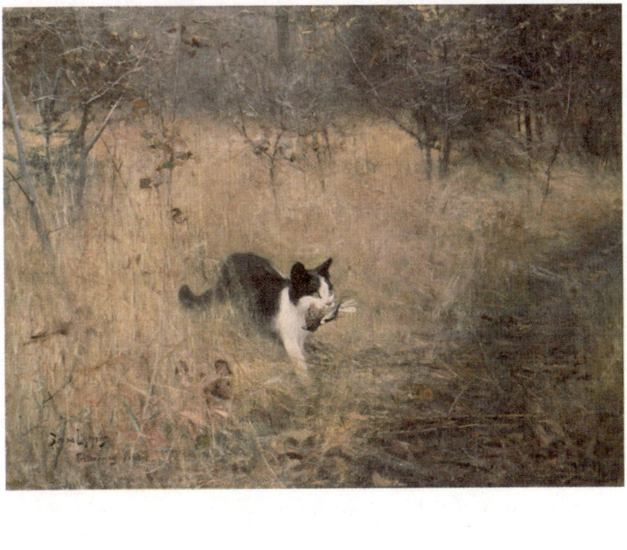

badly against one of the castors of the table. I could not see nor hear any thing for some minutes. When I came to myself, I found your dear mother holding me, and wiping my face with her own nice handkerchief wet in cold water. My right fore-paw was badly bruised, and that troubles me very much about washing my face, and about writing. But the worst of all is the condition of my nose. Everybody laughs who sees me, and I do not blame them; it is twice as large as it used to be, and I begin to be seriously afraid it will never return to its old shape. This will be a dreadful affliction: for who does not know that the nose is the chief beauty of a cat's face? I have got very tired of hearing the story of my fall told to all the people who come in. They laugh as if they would kill themselves at it, especially when I do not manage to get under the table before they look to see how my nose is.

Except for this I should have written to you before, and would write more now, but my paw aches badly, and one of my eyes is nearly closed from the swelling of my nose: so I must say goodbye.

> Your affectionate Pussy.

P. S. I told you about Caesar, did I not, in my last letter? Of course I do not venture out of the house in my present plight, so I have not seen him except from the window.

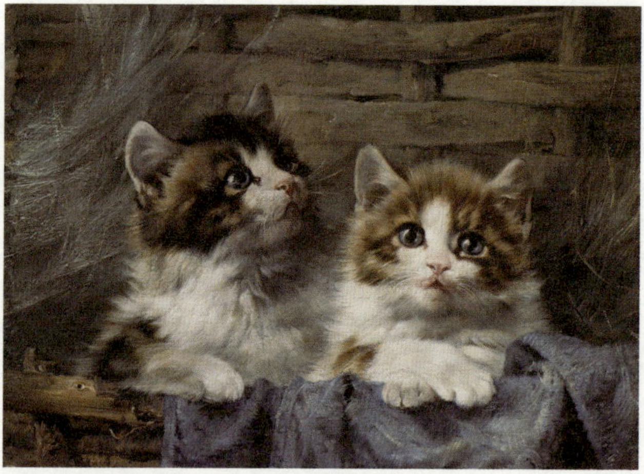

## 第五封信

我亲爱的海伦：

我肯定你必然十分好奇为什么过去两个星期我都没有给你写信，但等你知道我都经历了些什么后，你就只会庆幸我还能活着给你写信了。昨天，我听到你妈妈说她没有把我身上发生的事情写信告诉你，我很高兴，因为那些事肯定会令你不开心。不过现在一切都过去了，我很快就能恢复如初，我觉得你会愿意听听来龙去脉。

在上封信里，我跟你说过那只新搬来的住在纳尔逊家的黑猫恺撒，也跟你说过我很想认识他。我的鼻子一能见人，迪金森法官的猫——她是个善良

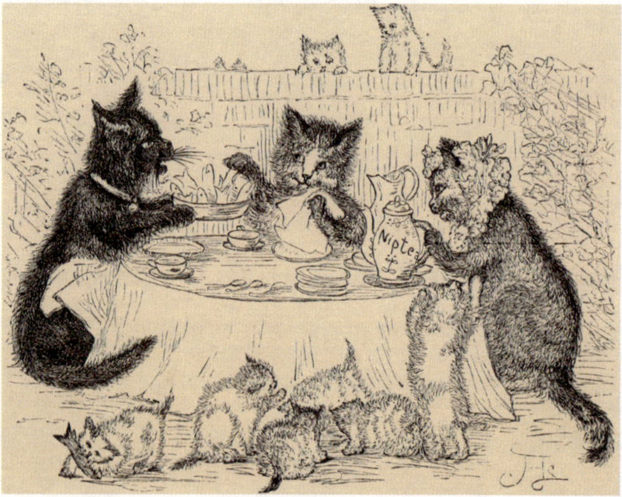
Nipte

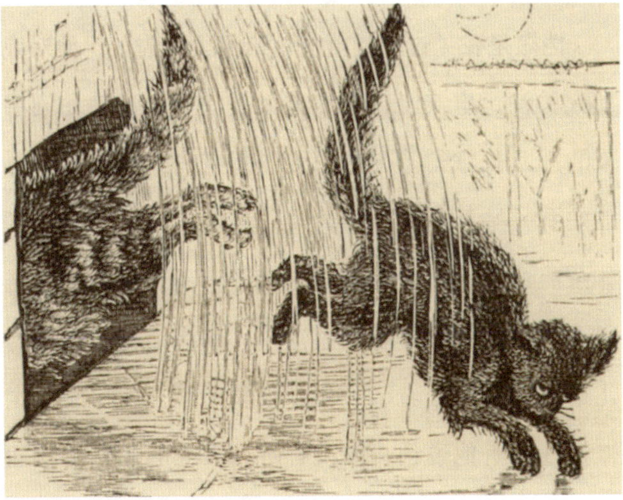

热情的老家伙，虽然有点儿蠢——就邀请我去喝茶，同时，她也邀请了恺撒。其他所有猫也都受到了邀请。他们会稍晚一些，在夜深时过去，一起享受一个大型聚会，在法官家的大谷仓里追猎老鼠。

恺撒是我见过的最英俊、最温柔的猫了。他对我十分关注，事实上，有点儿太关注了。从磨坊河谷来的那几只饿得半死的可怜猫里有一只因此而十分嫉妒我，她扑到我身上，咬住我的耳朵。最后我的耳朵流血了，聚会因此而结束了。不过恺撒把我送回了家，所以我并不在意这事。到家后，我们在育儿室窗户下面坐着聊天聊了很长时间。我一直都全神贯注地听他说话，都没有听到头上的窗户被玛丽给打开了，所以突然之间一整桶水从天而降浇到我们身上。我们两个都被吓坏了。我太惊讶了，一下子六神无主，都没有向恺撒道晚安，便直接从旁边地下室的窗户跳了进去。

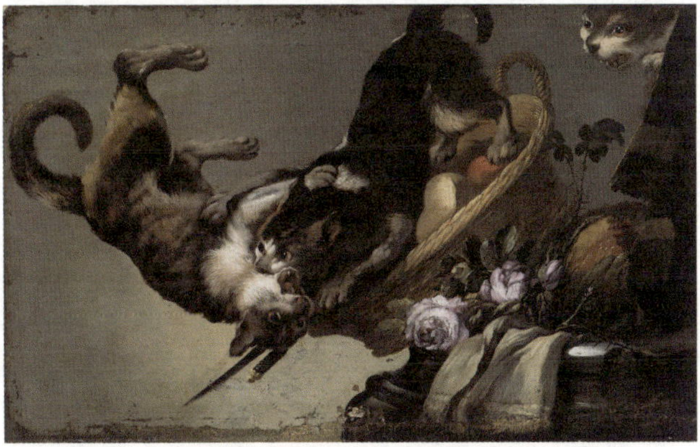

啊，我亲爱的海伦，我真不知道后来是怎么回事。我没有如同预料的一般落到卷心菜上——上一次我在地下室里的时候就看到那些卷心菜在窗户正下方的。我发现自己陷入了某种可怕的、软绵绵的、滑腻腻的、黏糊糊的东西里，不断下沉、下沉。本来这东西一瞬间就可能将我淹没，令我窒息，不过幸运的是，在下沉的时候，我感到一侧有什么硬东西，便努力伸出爪子抓了过去。事实上那是水桶的桶壁，我成功地把一只爪子探出了水桶边缘。我就吊在那里，时间一分钟一分钟地过去，我越来越虚弱，而那可怕的东西不断地往我眼睛和耳朵里面灌，那东西的气味古怪，呛得我喘不过气来。我用尽全力大声叫，发出的声音并不很大，因为我一张开嘴，那东西就会顺着我的胡子往我嘴里流。我呼唤恺撒，他悲痛万分地站在窗户边。我努力向他解释发生了什么事情，恳求他尽量大声叫，因为如果没有人及时过来把我捞出去，我肯定会死的。起初，他坚持要跳下来亲自帮我，但我告诉他这会是最愚蠢的做法，如果他这么做的话，我们两个肯定都会被淹死的。所以他用最大的声音喵喵叫，我们两个一起叫，声音挺大的，足足叫了几分钟，然后开始有窗户被打开了。我听到你祖父咒骂着，丢了一根木头出去砸恺撒。幸运的是，恺撒离房子很近，木头没有砸到他。最后，你祖父终于下楼来了，打开了后门，恺撒很害怕，便溜走了。因此，我之后就总觉得他没那么好了，尽管我们依然是非常好的朋友。

我听到他跑掉，在一段距离外说他很抱歉、不能帮我的忙了，我的勇气彻底瓦解了。再过一会儿，我就会滑下桶沿，沉到桶底。不过，幸运的是，你的祖父注意到我的叫声有些奇怪，便打开了地下室楼梯顶端的门，嘴里还说："我相信那猫肯定在这儿遇上麻烦了。"然后，我聚起力气，发出了更凄惨的叫声。我真希望我能够大声说:"是啊,就是啊,我要淹死了,不知道是淹在什么里面,但这东西比水糟糕多了!"

不过,你祖父还是明白了,他提着一盏灯走了下来。一看到我,他就把灯放到了地下室的地上,笑得几乎挪不动脚步。我认为这是我听过的最残酷的声音。如果我当时不是在地狱门口,我肯定会笑话他的,尽管我的眼睛当中都是那可怕的东西,我也能看到你祖父戴着红色睡帽,没有戴假牙,样子十分好笑。他冲着站在楼梯顶上的玛丽和你妈妈喊道:"下来,下来,猫掉到肥皂桶里了!"然后他又笑了。

玛丽和你妈妈都大笑着走下楼梯,甚至你那亲爱的和蔼的妈妈也在大笑,我从来都不相信她会笑话处于如此麻烦境地当中的家伙。起初,他们似乎不知道该怎么办,谁也不想碰我。我开始担心我会在他们的注视下淹死,因为我比他们都清楚自己抓了

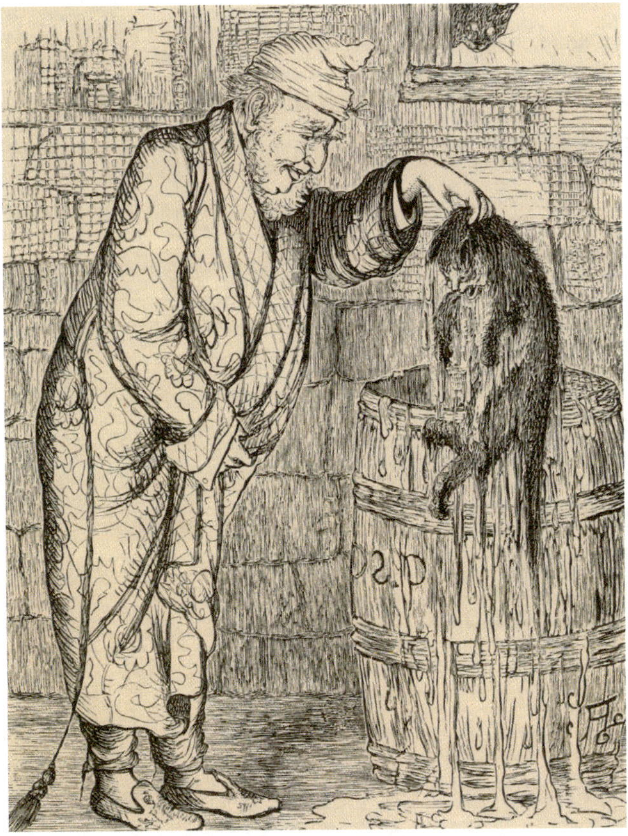

那么久桶沿之后现在有多虚弱。最后,你祖父骂出了他的那句口头禅——你知道我说的是哪句,就是他觉得别人非常可怜的时候总会骂出的那句——然后,拎着我的后颈将我提了出来。他尽量伸长胳膊,让我远离他,因为我腿上和尾巴上的肥皂液正哗哗地往下流。

他把我拎到了厨房里面,放在房间中央的地板上,然后,他们三个围着我站着,又笑了起来。他们的笑声太大了,把厨娘给吵醒了。厨娘一手拿着锡烛台、一手拎着椅子跑了出来,她以为是有劫匪闯了进来呢。最后,你亲爱的妈妈说:"可怜的小猫啊,你这样痛苦,我们还笑你真是不好。"(我已经这么认为很长时间了。)"玛丽,拿个小盆来,我们唯一能做的就是给她洗个澡了。"

我听到这话,几乎都希望他们任由我淹死在肥皂液里了,因为如果有什么东西能让我怕得要死的话，那便是水了。不过，我太虚弱了，没有办法反抗。他们把我浸到了装满了冰冷的水的澡盆里，然后玛丽便开始用她那硕大而粗糙的手揉搓我。我得告诉你，玛丽的手和你的手或你妈妈的手截然不同。看到涌出来的白色泡沫，他们又笑了起来。不到两分钟，整个澡盆里的水就都变成白色的了，就像我们经常一起去磨坊那里看到的水车下的水的颜色。

你能想象我的眼睛有多痛吗？有一次，有一块牛排从烤架上掉到了煤上，我为了弄到牛排，结果烫伤了爪子。但那疼痛和此刻比起来，简直什么都不是。若我告诉你，他们换了十次水才把我皮毛里的肥皂洗干净，你肯定很难相信。这时，我浑身发冷，精疲力竭，一动也不能动，他们都觉得我会死掉的。但是你妈妈用你的一件旧法兰绒衬裙将我裹了起来，在火炉后面给我安置了一张舒服的床。这时，甚至玛丽都开始可怜我了，尽管她起初非常生气，给我

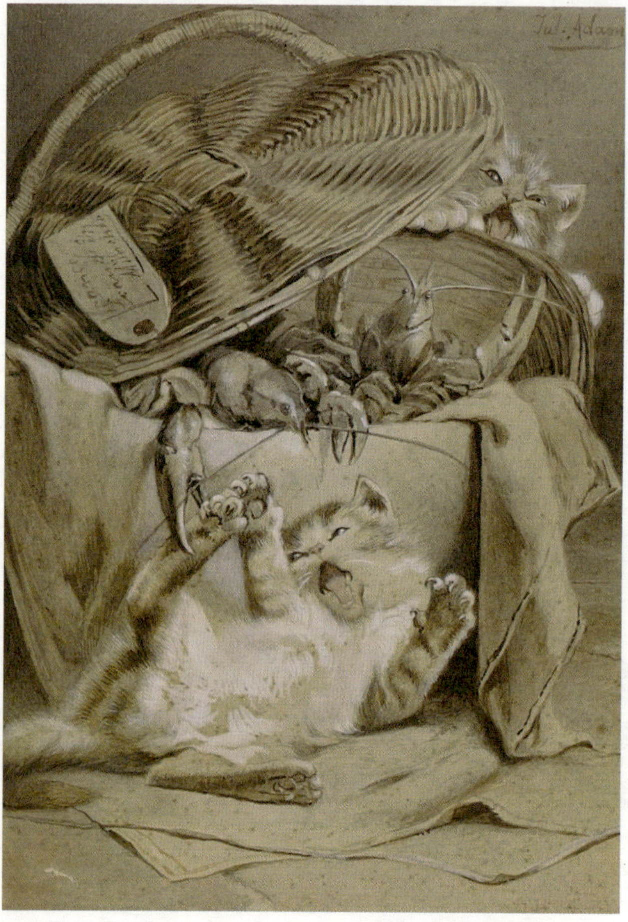
Jul. Adam

洗澡的时候，用的力气太大，弄得我很疼，现在她说："你不过是只可怜的小猫啊，如果小主人回来的时候发现你死了，我也会觉得难过的。"

所以，你看，你对我的爱确实对我有帮助，即便你离我很远。我非常怀疑，如果不是因为你，他们是否会费这么多的心思照顾我，帮我战胜这场伤痛。但是我必须就此搁笔，下封信再说了。我还不够强壮，没有办法一次写两个小时。

        爱你的小猫

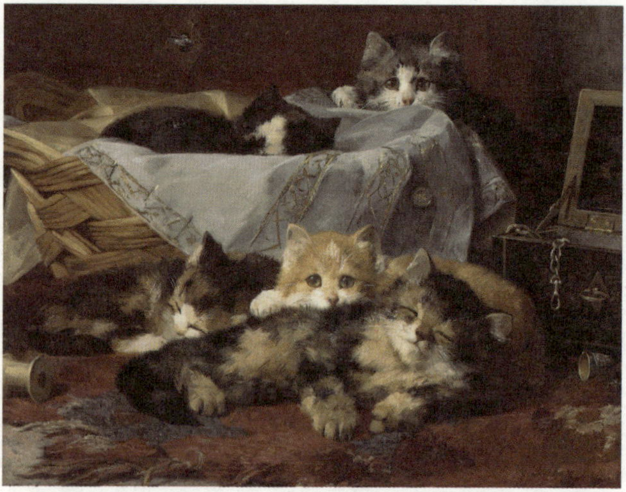

# V

My Dear Helen,

I am sure you must have wondered why I have not written to you for the last two weeks, but when you hear what I have been through, you will only wonder that I am alive to write to you at all. I was very glad to hear your mother say, yesterday, that she had not written to you about what had happened to me, because it would make you so unhappy. But now that it is all over, and I am in a fair way to be soon as well as ever, I think you will like to hear the whole story.

In my last letter I told you about the new black cat,

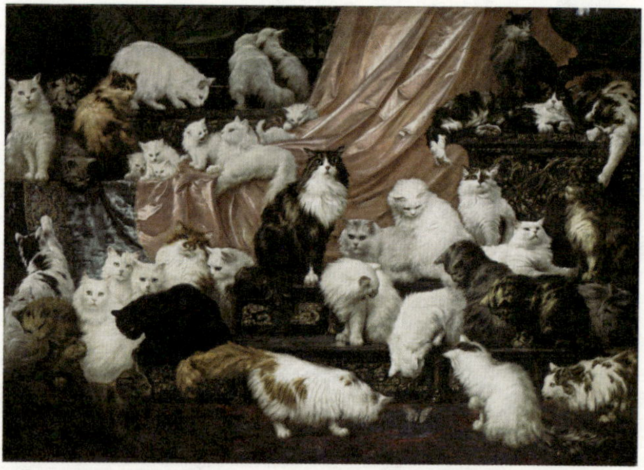

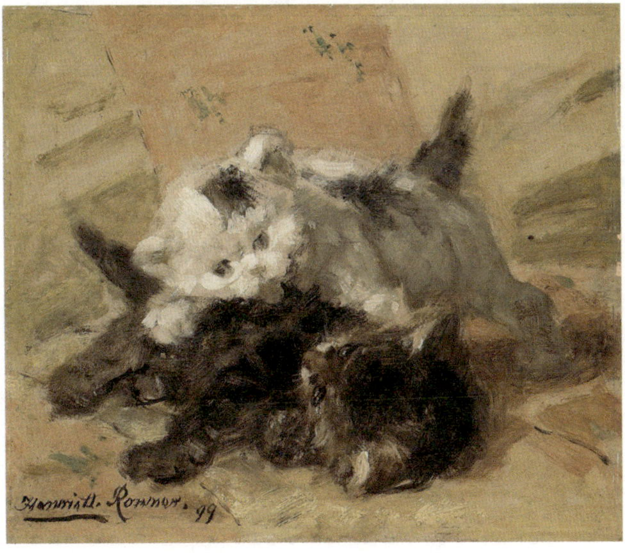

Caesar, who had come to live in the Nelson house, and how anxious I was to know him. As soon as my nose was fit to be seen, Judge Dickinson's cat, who is a good, hospitable old soul, in spite of her stupidity, invited me to tea, and asked him too. All the other cats were asked to come later in the evening, and we had a grand frolic, hunting rats in the Judge's great barn.

Caesar is certainly the handsomest and most gentlemanly cat I ever saw. He paid me great attention: in fact, so much, that one of those miserable half-starved cats from Mill Valley grew so jealous that she flew at me and bit my ear till it bled, which broke up the party. But Caesar went home with me, so I did not care; then we sat and talked a long time under the nursery window. I was so much occupied in what he was saying, that I did not hear Mary open the window overhead, and was therefore terribly frightened when there suddenly came down on us a whole pailful of water. I was so startled that I lost all presence of mind; and without bidding him good-night, I jumped directly into the cellar window by which we were sitting.

Oh, my dear Helen, I can never give you any idea of what followed. Instead of coming down as I expected to on the cabbages, which were just under that window the last time I was in the cellar, I found myself sinking, sinking, into some horrible soft, slimy, sticky substance, which in an instant more would have closed over my head, and suffocated me; but, fortunately, as I sank, I felt something hard at one side, and making a great effort, I caught on it with my claws. It proved to be the side of a barrel, and I succeeded in getting one paw over the edge of it. There I hung, growing weaker and weaker every minute, with this frightful stuff running into my eyes and ears, and choking

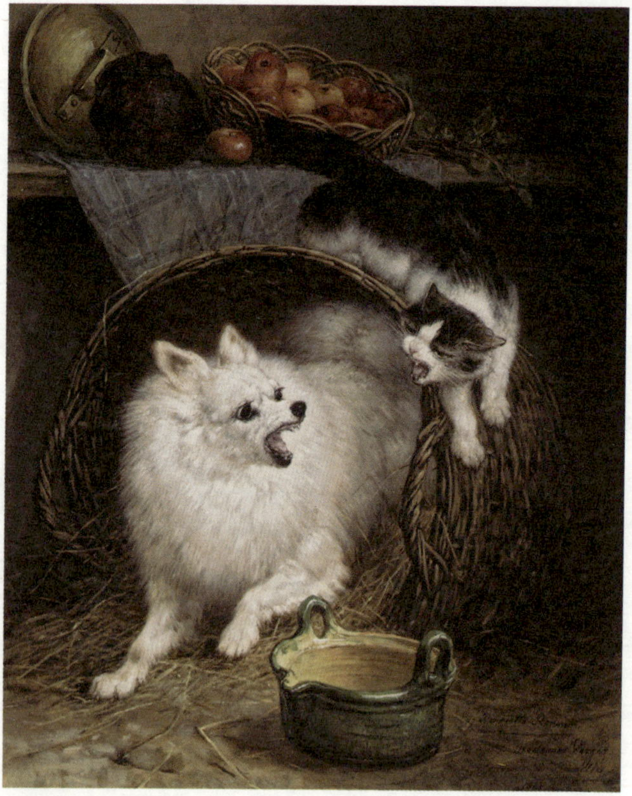

me with its bad smell. I mewed as loud as I could, which was not very loud, for whenever I opened my mouth the stuff trickled into it off my whiskers; but I called to Caesar, who stood in great distress at the window, and explained to him, as well as I could, what had happened to me, and begged him to call as loudly as possible; for if somebody did not come very soon, and take me out, I should certainly die. He insisted, at first, on jumping down to help me himself; but I told him that would be the most foolish thing he could do; if he did, we should certainly both be drowned. So he began to meow at the top of his voice, and between his mewing and mine, there was noise enough for a few minutes; then windows began to open, and I heard your grandfather swearing and throwing out a stick of wood at Caesar; fortunately he was so near the house that it did not hit him. At last your grandfather came downstairs, and opened the back door; and Caesar was so frightened that he ran away, for which I have never thought so well of him since, though we are still very good friends.

When I heard him running off, and calling back to me, from a distance, that he was so sorry he could not help me, my courage began to fail, and in a moment more, I should have let go of the edge of the barrel, and sunk to the bottom; but luckily your grandfather noticed that there was something very strange about my mewing, and opened the door at the head of the cellar stairs, saying, "I do believe the cat is in some trouble down here." Then I made a great effort and mewed still more piteously. How I wished I could call out and say, "Yes, indeed, I am; drowning to death, in I'm sure I don't know what, but something a great deal worse than water!"

However, he understood me as it was, and came down

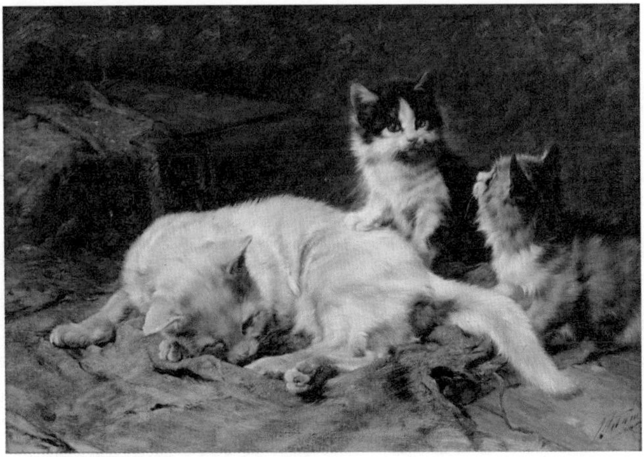

with a lamp. As soon as he saw me, he set the lamp down on the cellar bottom, and laughed so that he could hardly move. I thought this was the most cruel thing I ever heard of. If I had not been, as it were, at death's door, I should have laughed at him, too, for even with my eyes full of that dreadful stuff, I could see that he looked very funny in his red night-cap, and without his teeth. He called out to Mary, and your mother, who stood at the head of the stairs, "Come down, come down; here's the cat in the soft-soap barrel!" and then he laughed again, and they both came down the stairs laughing, even your dear kind mother, who I never could have believed would laugh at any one in such trouble. They did not seem to know what to do at first; nobody wanted to touch me; and I began to be afraid I should drown while they stood looking at me, for I knew much better than they could how weak I was from holding on to the edge of the barrel so long. At last your grandfather swore that oath of his, —you know the one I mean, the one he always swears when he is very sorry for anybody, —and lifted me out by the nape of my neck, holding me as far off from him as he could, for the soft soap ran off my legs and tail in streams.

He carried me up into the kitchen, and put me down in the middle of the floor, and then they all stood round me, and laughed again, so loud that they waked up the cook, who came running out of her bedroom with her tin candlestick and a chair in her hand, thinking that robbers were breaking in. At last your dear mother said, "Poor pussy, it is too bad to laugh at you, when you are in such pain." (I had been thinking so for some time.) "Mary, bring the small washtub. The only thing we can do is to wash her."

When I heard this, I almost wished they had left me to

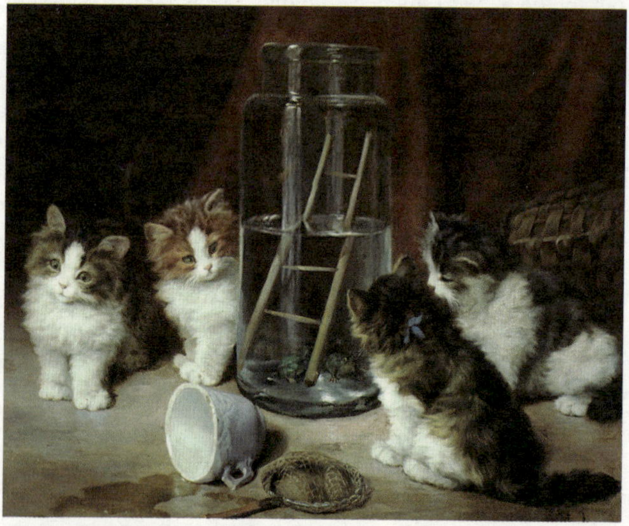

drown in the soft soap; for if there is any thing of which I have a mortal dread, it is water. However, I was too weak to resist; and they plunged me in all over, into the tub full of ice-cold water, and Mary began to rub me with her great rough hands, which, I assure you, are very different from yours and your mother's. Then they all laughed again to see the white lather it made; in two minutes the whole tub was as white as the water under the mill-wheel that you and I have so often been together to see.

You can imagine how my eyes smarted. I burnt my paws once in getting a piece of beefsteak out of the coals where it had fallen off the gridiron, but the pain of that was nothing to this. You will hardly believe me when I tell you that they had to empty the tub and fill it again ten times before the soap was all washed out of my fur. By that time I was so cold and exhausted, that I could not move, and they

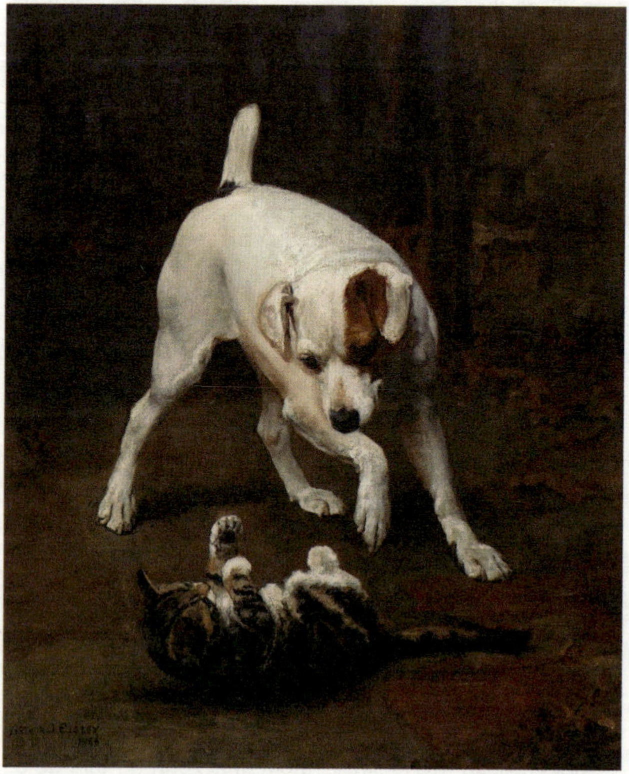

began to think I should die. But your mother rolled me up in one of your old flannel petticoats, and made a nice bed for me behind the stove. By this time even Mary began to seem sorry for me, though she was very cross at first, and hurt me much more than she need to in washing me; now she said, "You're nothing but a poor beast of a cat, to be sure; but it's meself that would be sorry to have the little mistress come back, and find ye kilt."

So you see your love for me did me service, even when you were so far away. I doubt very much whether they would have ever taken the trouble to nurse me through this sickness, except for your sake. But I must leave the rest for my next letter. I am not strong enough yet to write more than two hours at a time.

Your affectionate Pussy.

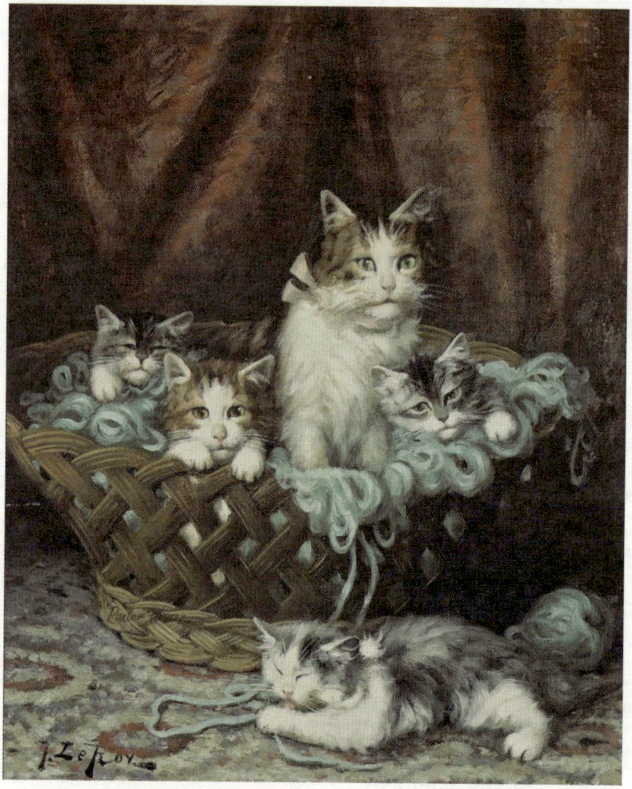

## 第六封信

我亲爱的海伦：

接着给你讲述上封信没讲完的事情。

你应该可以想象，那天晚上，我一点儿都没睡，甚至连个"猫盹"都没有打。人们经常说"猫盹"，不过我并不知道猫盹和男人或女人打的盹之间有什么区别。我整夜都抖个不停，只要一动就疼得厉害。第二天一早，你祖父下楼来，看到我的样子后，又骂了粗话，还是那一句。我们都很清楚他那么骂粗话是什么意思，那意味着他会尽一切所能来帮助你，也是他太难过了，难过到害怕被别人看出来。你还记得那次你被拔掉那颗叠长在一起的大牙、他给了

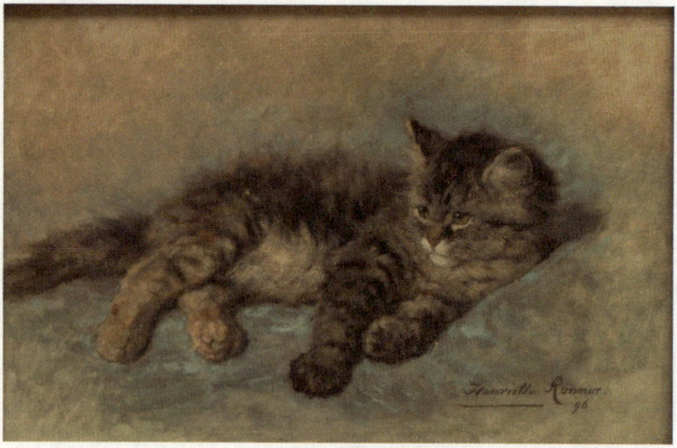
Henriette Ronner
96

你五块钱时,是怎么骂粗话的吗?好吧,他把我抱在怀里,将我带到餐厅里。天气很冷,但是炉膛里面有木炭烧着,很舒服。玛丽正在摆早餐。他用粗哑的声音对玛丽说:"喂,玛丽,你到阁楼里面去把摇篮拿下来。"

我看到玛丽的脸一下子变了色,尽管很难受,我还是情不自禁地笑了。那情形能让任何一只猫都笑起来。

"先生,你不是说,你要把这只猫放到摇篮里面吧?"

"你按我说的办。"他说,用的是他最吓人的声调,那声音会让你也感到害怕。我自己都感到害怕了,尽管他一直轻抚着我的头,说:"可怜的小猫啊,听话,可怜的小猫啊,躺着别动。"几分钟后,玛丽将摇篮搬了下来,砰的一声放到了壁炉旁边,那声音大得吓人,我都担心摇篮是不是被摔坏了。你知道的,她不高兴的时候,总是砰砰地摔东西,不过我真不明白这么做有什么好处。你祖父用查雷冬天披的毯子和一个旧枕头把摇篮铺得舒舒服服，接着将我放到了摇篮里，我就像是被包在你的衬裙里那样被包了起来。你妈妈回到屋里看到我的时候，大笑不止，就和看到我在肥皂桶里面时笑的差不多。她说："哎呀，父亲，你可年纪不小了，不适合玩猫的摇篮了。"老人家也笑了，笑得眼泪都顺着红脸颊往下流。"好吧，"他说，"我告诉你一件事：我会一直玩这个游戏，直到这只猫康复。"然后他到楼上，拿下了一瓶东西，那东西又软又滑，有点儿像是猪油，他把那东西涂在我的眼睛上，令我感觉好了很多。然后，他又给了我一些牛奶，还在里面掺上了他最好的白兰地：那可真是难以下咽，但是我非常理解人们说的话，我相信如果没有喝下那种东西，我就永远都不会好起来了。吃完早餐，我想要起来走走，但是我的右爪完全不能动。最初，他们以为它是断掉了，最后发现只是扭伤了，但必须用绷带裹

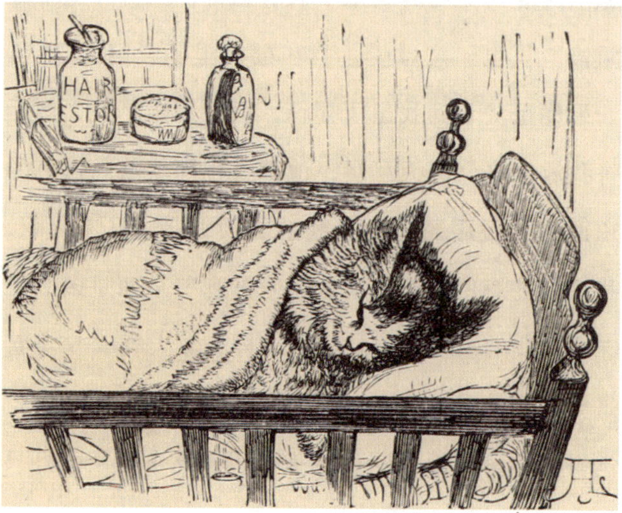
HAIR

起来。绷带湿漉漉的,上面沾了一些味道很不好的东西,最初的一两天让我觉得很难受。猫的鼻子对气味比人类敏感很多,但我还是慢慢习惯了那味道,那东西对我受伤的瘸爪子大有益处,就算味道难闻两倍,我也愿意忍受。我在摇篮里躺了整整三天,如果你祖父看到我出了摇篮,就会厉声骂我,然后将我放回去。每天早晨,他都会把那软软的白色的东西涂到我眼睛上,给我的腿换绷带。还有,啊,我亲爱的海伦,还要说说我吃的那些东西是多么美味啊!我的饭食几乎就和人一样:做人类——不管是男人还是女人——一定是件非常美妙的事情!我觉得,我再也不会愿意在猫舍里面吃东西,而且只能吃些没有人想要的剩饭。

在我不得不待在摇篮里期间,有两件事情困扰着我。一件是所有来拜访你妈妈的人只要看到我,就会笑个不停;另一件便是我听到可怜的恺撒一直绕着

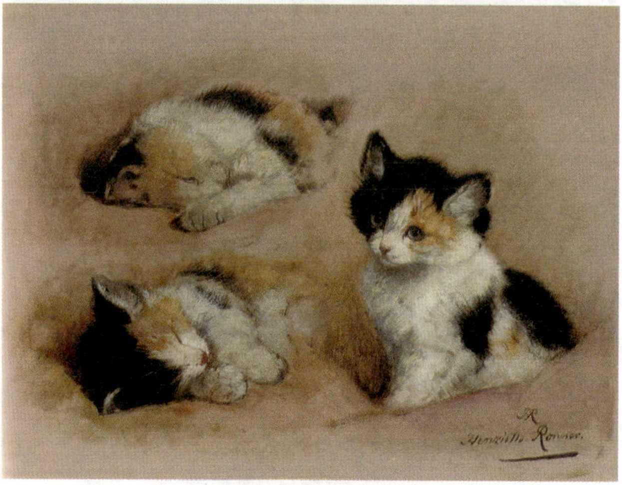

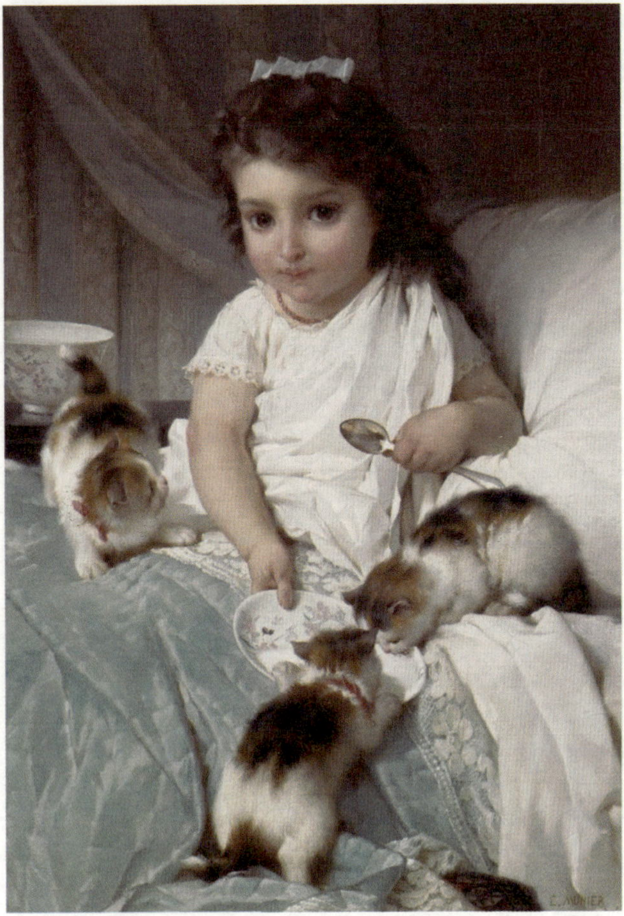

咱们家叫唤，用最大的声音呼唤我，我知道他以为我死了。我费尽心思想让你和蔼的妈妈注意到他的叫声，因为我知道她肯定会愿意让恺撒进来看我的，但是我没有办法让她明白我的意思。我觉得她肯定认为这只是某只饥饿的流浪猫的正常叫声。我注意很久了，人类并没有察觉到一只猫的叫声和另一只猫的叫声有什么区别，实际上它们就和人的声音一样区别很大的。恺撒的声音是我听过的最美妙最深沉的。在我身体康复到能够走到厨房之后，有一天，他从送肉来的屠夫家男孩的两条腿之间溜了进来。但我还没来得及对他说一个字，玛丽就拿着扫把飞奔过去，将他赶了出去。不过，他看到我还活着，这就够了。我很担心自己还得过段日子才能再度见到他，因为他们根本不让我出门，而且我腿上的绷带也还没有拆开。摇篮被搬回到了楼上，我现在睡在火炉后面，查雷的毯子铺在我身下。今天我听你

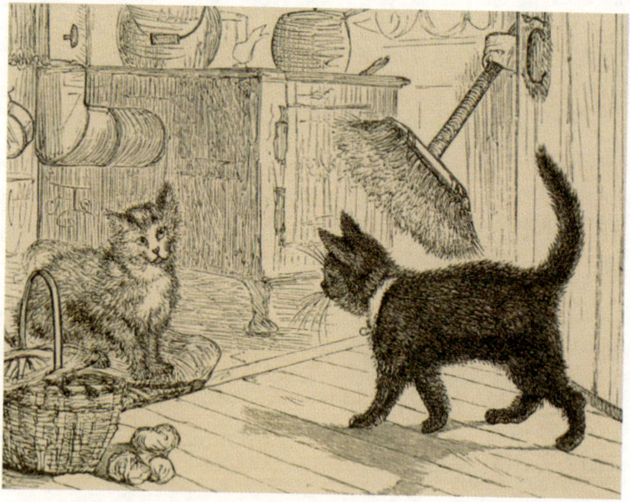

妈妈说，她确信猫得了风湿病。我不知道风湿病是什么，但是我相信我得了，因为我走路的时候会浑身疼。我觉得自己的样子就像是比尔·雅各布的那只老猫，人们都说那只猫比镇上最老的老人年纪还要大，当然，这肯定是胡扯。

我最担心的是我的毛，我的毛成块成块地往下掉，我脖子后面，就是他们将我拎出肥皂桶的时候拎的那个地方，秃了一块，那秃癞有你手掌的一半那么大。我每次清理自己，都会落得满嘴毛，这实在很让人讨厌。今天我听你祖父说，他认为他需要在猫身上试试某某太太的防脱发秘方了，这话引得所有人都大笑起来。我则以最快的速度从房间里跑了出去，而他们笑得更加厉害了。我会在这两天继续给你写信，告诉你我恢复得如何。我希望你能尽快回家。

            爱你的小猫

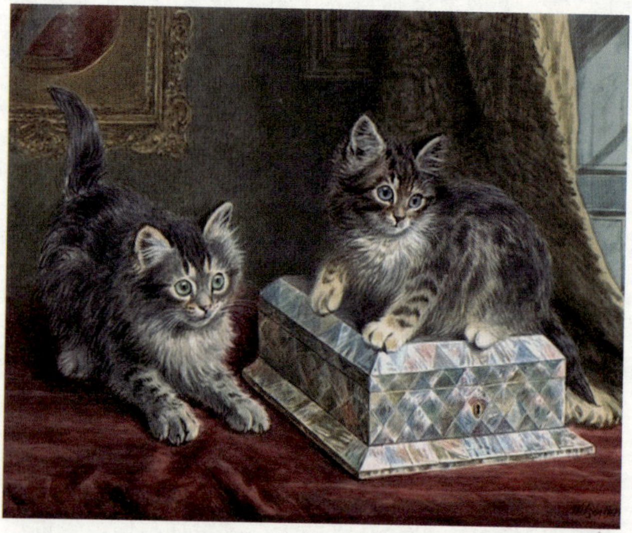

# VI

My Dear Helen,

I will begin where I left off in my last letter.

As you may imagine, I did not get any sleep that night, not even so much as a cat's nap, as people say, though how cat's naps differ from men's and women's naps, I don't know. I shivered all night, and it hurt me terribly whenever I moved. Early in the morning your grandfather came downstairs, and when he saw how I looked, he swore again, that same oath: we all know very well what it means when he swears in that way: it means that he is going to do all he can for you, and is so sorry, that he is afraid of seeming too

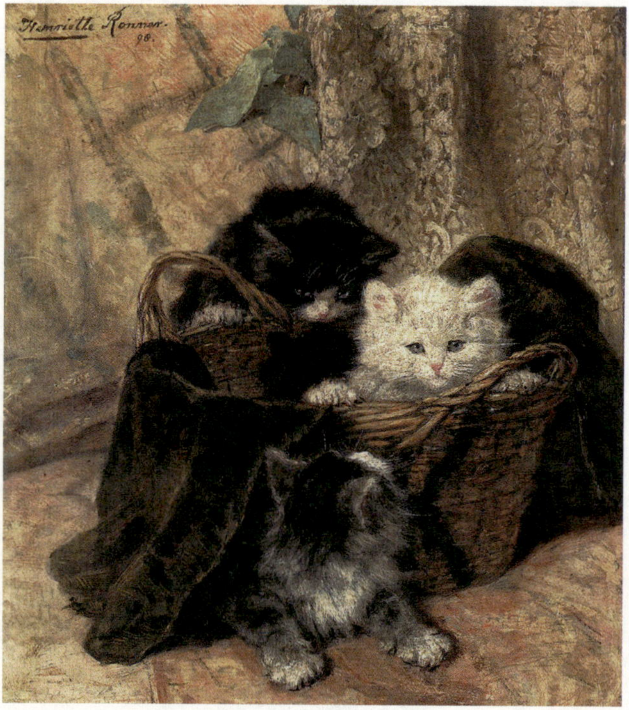
Henriette Ronner
98.

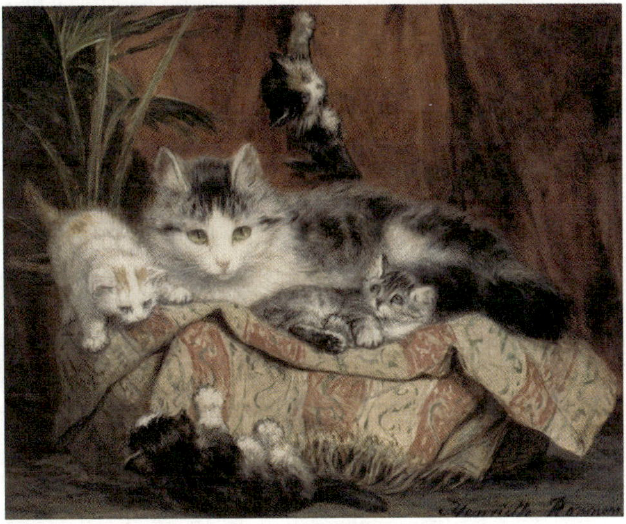

sorry. Don't you remember when you had that big double tooth pulled out, and he gave you five dollars, how he swore then? Well, he took me up in his arms, and carried me into the dining-room; it was quite cool; there was a nice wood fire on the hearth, and Mary was setting the table for breakfast. He said to her in a very gruff voice, "Here you, Mary, you go up into the garret and bring down the cradle."

Sick as I was, I could not help laughing at the sight of her face. It was enough to make any cat laugh.

"You don't ever mean to say, sir, as you're going to put that cat into the cradle."

"You do as I tell you," said he, in that most awful tone of his, which always makes you so afraid. I felt afraid myself, though all the time he was stroking my head, and saying, "Poor pussy, there, poor pussy, lie still." In a few minutes Mary came down with the cradle, and set it down by the fire with such a bang that I wondered it did not break. You know she always bangs things when she is cross, but I never could see what good it does. Then your grandfather made up a nice bed in the cradle, out of Charlie's winter blanket and an old pillow, and laid me down in it, all rolled up as I was in your petticoat. When your mother came into the room she laughed almost as hard as she did when she saw me in the soft-soap barrel, and said, "Why, father, you are rather old to play cat's cradle!" The old gentleman laughed at this, till the tears ran down his red cheeks. "Well," he said, "I tell you one thing: the game will last me till that poor cat gets well again." Then he went upstairs, and brought down a bottle of something very soft and slippery, like lard, and put it on my eyes, and it made them feel much better. After that he gave me some milk into which he had put some of his very best brandy: that was pretty hard to get down, but I understood enough of what they had said, to be sure that if I did not take something of the kind I should never get well. After breakfast I tried to walk, but my right paw was entirely useless. At first they thought it was broken, but finally decided that it was only sprained, and must be bandaged. The bandages were wet with something which smelled so badly it made me feel very sick, for the first day or two. Cats' noses are much more sensitive to smells than people's are; but I grew used to it, and it did my poor lame paw so much good that I would have borne it if it had smelled twice as badly. For three days I had to lie all the time in the cradle: if your grandfather caught me out of it, he would swear at me, and put me back again. Every morning he put the soft white stuff on my eyes, and changed the bandages on my leg. And, oh, my dear Helen, such good things as I had to eat! I had almost the same things for my dinner that the rest of them did: it must be a splendid thing to be a man or a woman! I do not think I shall ever again be contented to eat in the shed, and have only the old pieces which nobody wants.

Two things troubled me very much while I was confined to the cradle: one was that everybody who came in to see your mother laughed as if they never could stop, at the first sight of me; and the other was that I heard poor Caesar mewing all around the house, and calling me with all his might; and I knew he thought I was dead. I tried hard to make your kind mother notice his crying, for I knew she would be willing to let him come in and see me, but I could not make her understand. I suppose she thought it was only some common strolling cat who was hungry. I have always noticed that people do not observe any difference between one cat's voice and another's; now they really are just as

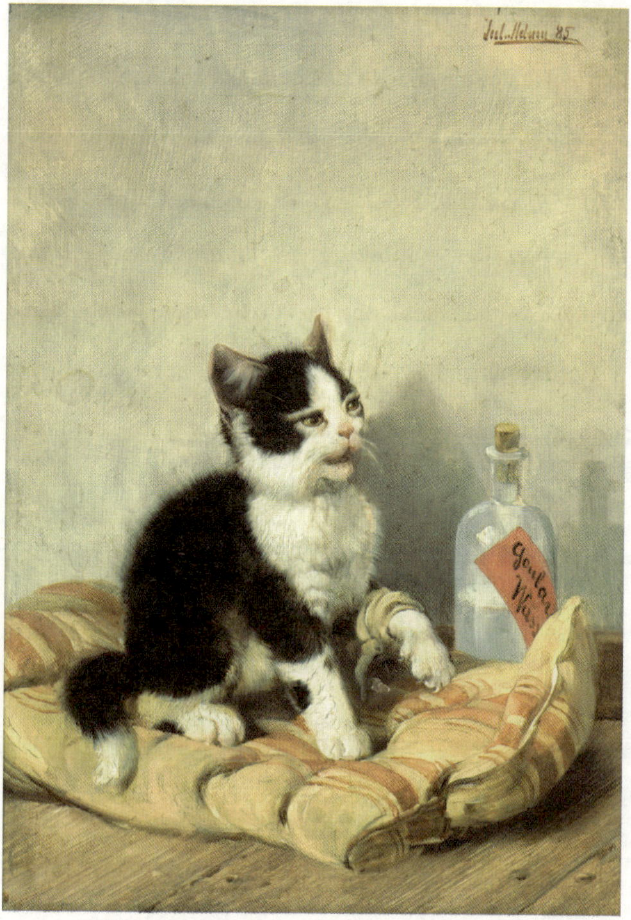

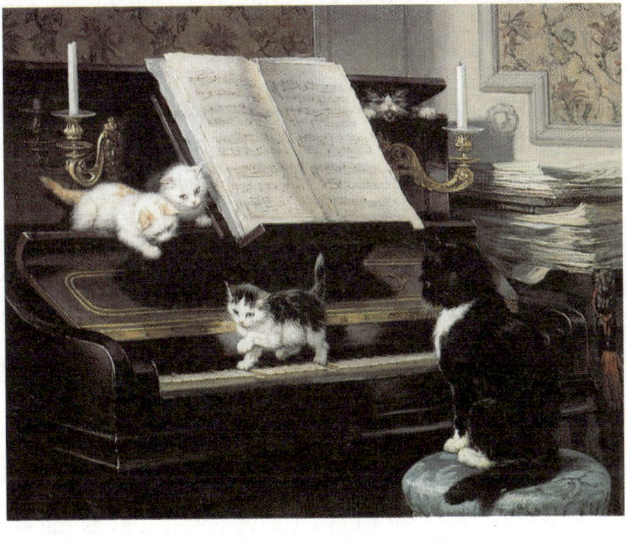

different as human voices. Caesar has one of the finest, deepest toned voices I ever heard. One day, after I got well enough to be in the kitchen, he slipped in, between the legs of the butcher's boy who was bringing in some meat; but before I had time to say one word to him, Mary flew at him with the broom, and drove him out. However, he saw that I was alive, and that was something. I am afraid it will be some days yet before I can see him again, for they do not let me go out at all, and the bandages are not taken off my leg. The cradle is carried upstairs, and I sleep on Charlie's blanket behind the stove. I heard your mother say today that she really believed the cat had the rheumatism. I do not know what that is, but I think I have got it: it hurts me all over when I walk, and I feel as if I looked like Bill Jacobs's old cat, who, they say, is older than the oldest man in town; but of course that must be a slander.

The thing I am most concerned about is my fur; it is coming off in spots: there is a bare spot on the back of my neck, on the place by which they lifted me up out of the soap barrel, half as large as your hand; and whenever I wash myself, I get my mouth full of hairs, which is very disagreeable. I heard your grandfather say today, that he believed he would try Mrs. Somebody's Hair Restorer on the cat, at which everybody laughed so that ran out of the room as fast as I could go, and then they laughed still harder. I will write you again in a day or two, and tell you how I am getting on. I hope you will come home soon.

                                    Your affectionate Pussy.

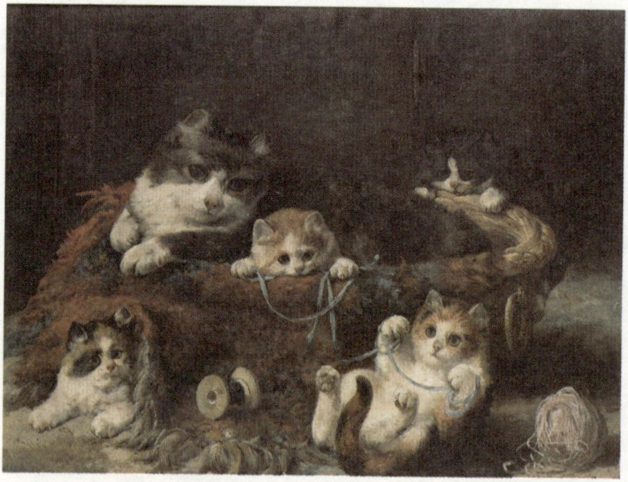

## 第七封信

我亲爱的海伦：

很高兴得知你下个星期就要回家了，自从知道这消息，我满脑子都想着这件事。

我在欢喜之余只有一个缺憾，那就是我很不愿意让你看到我现在的窘态。上封信里我跟你说过，我的毛开始脱落。你祖父在我身上试了好几种他自己的防脱发的东西，但是没有一点儿效果。我倒从没觉得这些东西会有效果，头发和毛是两种非常不同的东西，从一开始我就认为，把适用于人类头皮的东西涂在我的皮肤上没有什么用处，更别说那东西对人类的头皮也没有什么明显效果。依照你祖父

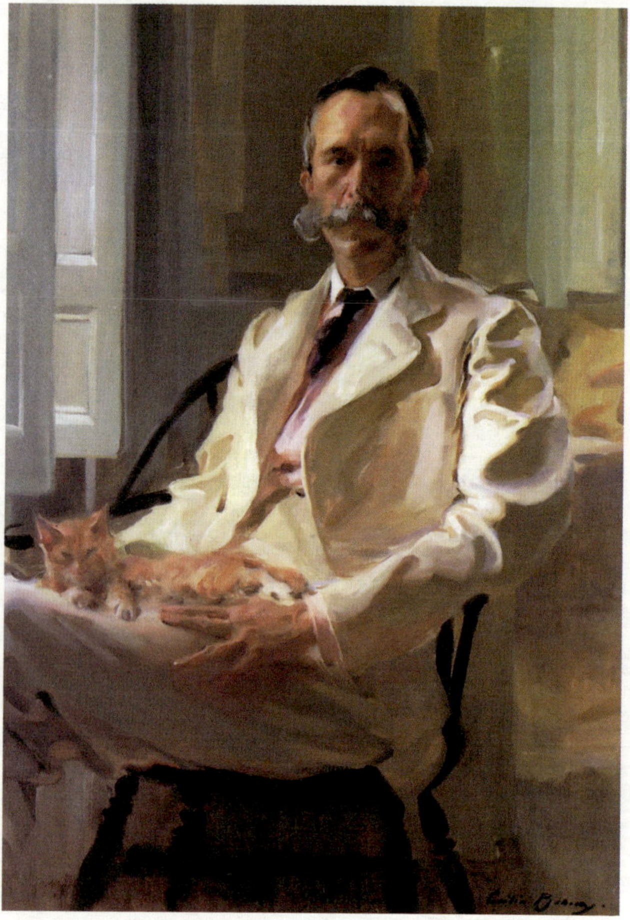

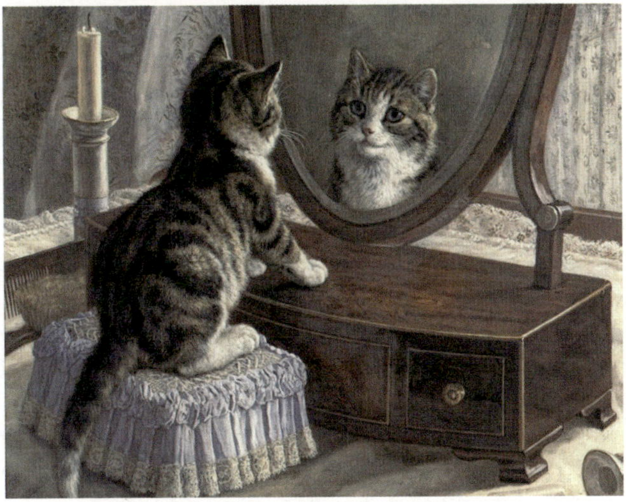

的头来做判断的话就是这样子的,你知道的,你祖父的头光光的,泛着粉色的光,就像是个婴儿的头一样。不过,他对我太好了,我愿意让他在我身上为所欲为。每天,他都给我擦一种新东西,味道一种比一种糟糕。带着这样的气味,我连走到距老鼠半英里范围内都绝对不可能,这就像是我开了一枪通知他们我来了,他们还没看到我,就已经早早闻到了我的气味。

如果没有我的皮毛的问题,那我是非常开心的,因为我感觉前所未有地好。我现在比你离家的时候胖了一倍。我努力接受今后的命运,不管我会变成什么样,不过我很难接受自己余生变成一只模样丑陋的猫。我不认为这个世界上有没长毛的猫。

今天早晨,你祖父坐着看着我,看了很长一段时间,他一边看一边摸着自己的下巴,最后说:"你们觉不觉得把猫的毛全剃掉会比较好?"听到这话,我难以自控地叫了起来。你妈妈说:"我相信我们在谈论小猫的时候她是听得懂的。"

我当然听得懂啊!怎么会听不懂呢?人们似乎从来都没有意识到猫也是有耳朵的。我常常想,如果他们意识到这一点,他们的言行就会谨慎许多许多。我曾经看到过很多次,他们把孩子赶出房间,却把我留了下来,我非常清楚,孩子们能注意到的或是能听明白的根本不及我一半多。在我和你一起生活之前,我在一些房子里面住过,如果我想,是能讲出些关于那些房子的奇怪故事的。

恺撒假装他喜欢我皮毛上露出一小块一小块粉色皮肤的样子,但是我知道他只是不想伤害我,因为就人的本性——我是说猫的本性——来说,谁也不会喜欢的。你看,我和人相处太久了,比和猫相处的时间多得多,我发现自己经常用到一些从猫嘴里说出来显得很奇怪的表达。但是你非常了解我,会

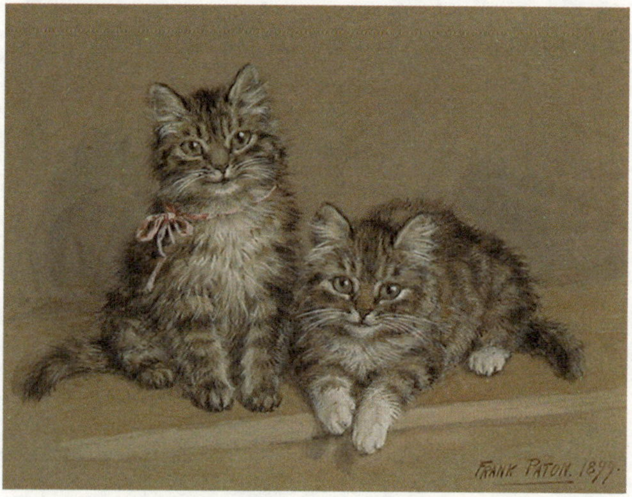
FRANK PATON. 1899.

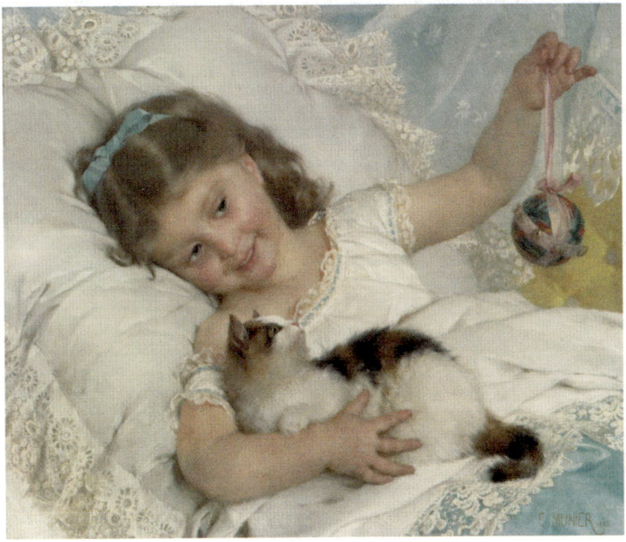

相信我说的一切都是毫不做作的。

现在,我亲爱的海伦,我希望我已经让你做好了心理准备,准备看到我极其吓人的样子。我只能相信你对我的爱不会因我不幸的样子而被全部抹杀。如果你真的没有过去那么爱我了,我会非常难过,但是我会一直爱你的。

爱你的小猫

# VII

My Dear Helen,

I am so glad to know that you are coming home next week, that I cannot think of any thing else.

There is only one drawback to my pleasure, and that is, I am so ashamed to have you see me in such a plight. I told you, in my last letter, that my fur was beginning to come off. Your grandfather has tried several things of his, which are said to be good for hair; but they have not had the least effect. For my part I don't see why they should; fur and hair are two very different things, and I thought at the outset there was no use in putting on my skin what was intended

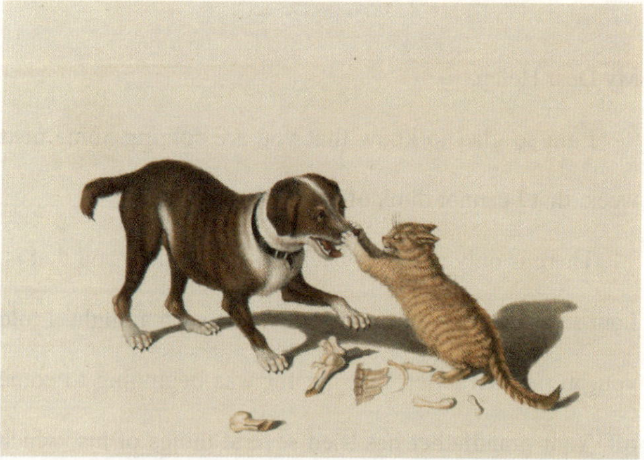

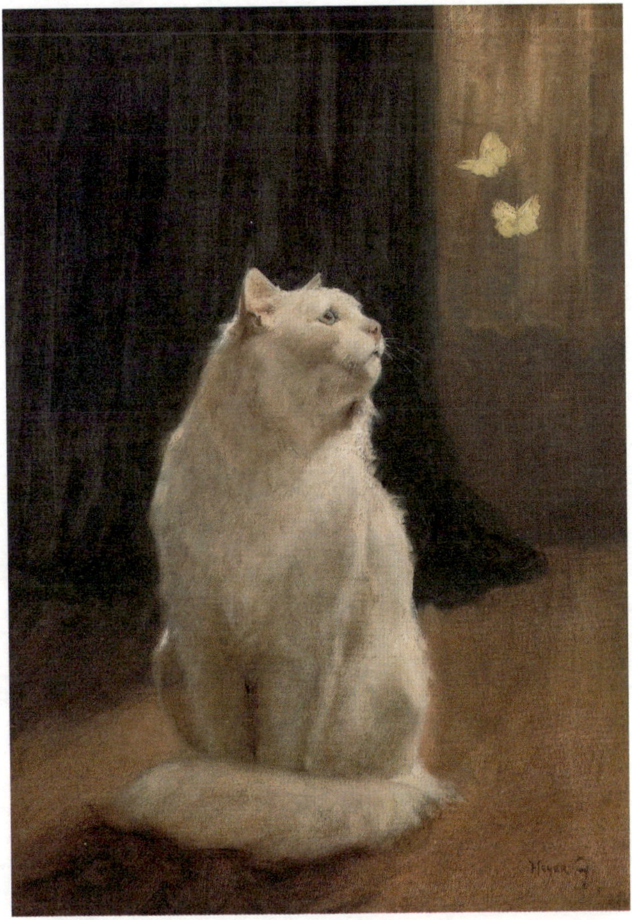

for the skin of human heads, and even on them don't seem to work any great wonders, if I can judge from your grandfather's head, which you know is as bald and pink and shiny as a baby's. However, he has been so good to me, that I let him do any thing he likes, and every day he rubs in some new kind of stuff, which smells a little worse than the last one. It is utterly impossible for me to get within half a mile of a rat or a mouse. I might as well fire off a gun to let them know I am coming, as to go about scented up so that they can smell me a great deal farther off than they can see me.

If it were not for this dreadful state of my fur, I should be perfectly happy, for I feel much better than I ever did before in my whole life, and am twice as fat as when you went away. I try to be resigned to whatever may be in store for me, but it is very hard to look forward to being a fright all the rest of one's days. I don't suppose such a thing was ever seen in the world as a cat without any fur.

This morning your grandfather sat looking at me for a long time and stroking his chin: at last he said, "Do you suppose it would do any good to shave the cat all over?" At this I could not resist the impulse to scream, and your mother said, "I do believe the creature knows whenever we speak about her."

Of course I do! Why in the world shouldn't I! People never seem to observe that cats have ears. I often think how much more careful they would be if they did. I have many a time to see them send children out of the room, and leave me behind, when I knew perfectly well that the children would neither notice nor understand half so much as I would. There are some houses in which I lived, before I came to live with you, about which I could tell strange stories if I chose.

Caesar pretends that he likes the looks of little spots of pink skin, here and there, in fur; but I know he only does it to save my feelings, for it isn't in human nature—I mean in cat's nature—that any one should. You see I spend so much more time in the society of men and women than of cats, that I find myself constantly using expressions which sound queerly in a cat's mouth. But you know me well enough to be sure that every thing I say is perfectly natural.

And now, my dear Helen, I hope I have prepared you to see me looking perfectly hideous. I only trust that your love for me will not be entirely killed by my unfortunate appearance. If you do seem to love me less, I shall be wretched, but I shall still be, always,

Your affectionate Pussy.

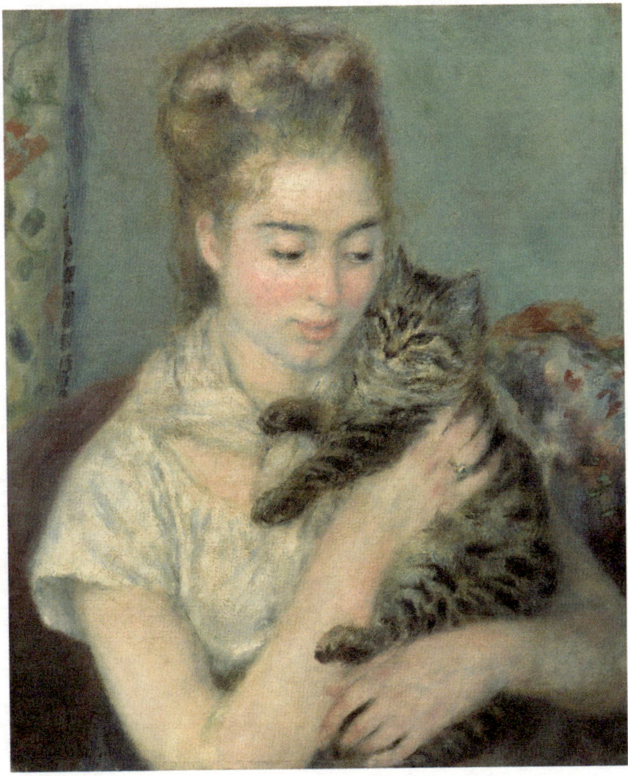

# 图书在版编目（CIP）数据

猫咪来信：汉英对照 / (美)海伦·亨特·杰克逊著；王秀莉译. — 西安：太白文艺出版社，2018.3
ISBN 978-7-5513-1339-1

Ⅰ.①猫… Ⅱ.①海…②王… Ⅲ.①英语 - 汉语 - 对照读物②童话 - 美国 - 近代 Ⅳ.① H319.4：I

中国版本图书馆CIP数据核字（2017）第289085号

## 猫咪来信
MAOMILAIXIN

| 作　　者 | 〔美〕海伦·亨特·杰克逊 |
|---|---|
| 译　　者 | 王秀莉 |
| 责任编辑 | 王婧姝 |
| 特约编辑 | 赵丽娟 |
| 整体设计 | 灵动视线 |
| 出版发行 | 陕西新华出版传媒集团 |
| | 太白文艺出版社（西安北大街147号　710003） |
| | 太白文艺出版社发行：029-87277748 |
| 经　　销 | 新华书店 |
| 印　　刷 | 北京旭丰源印刷技术有限公司 |
| 开　　本 | 787mm×1092mm　1/32 |
| 字　　数 | 70千字 |
| 印　　张 | 6.25 |
| 版　　次 | 2018年3月第1版　2018年3月第1次印刷 |
| 书　　号 | ISBN 978-7-5513-1339-1 |
| 定　　价 | 39.80元 |

版权所有　翻印必究
如有印装质量问题，可寄出版社印制部调换
联系电话：029-87250869